GEORGE JACOB HOLYOAKE

George Jacob Holyoake

GEORGE JACOB HOLYOAKE

A Study in the Evolution of a Victorian Radical

Lee E. Grugel

PORCUPINE PRESS

Philadephia 1976

First published 1976 by
PORCUPINE PRESS INC.
Philadelphia, Pennsylvania 19107

Library of Congress Cataloging in Publication Data

Grugel, Lee E   1940-
   George Jacob Holyoake.

   Bibliography: p.
   Includes index.
   1. Holyoake, George Jacob, 1817-1906. 2. Labor
and laboring classes--Great Britain--Biography.
3. Labor and laboring classes--Great Britain--Political
activity--History. 4. Great Britain--Social conditions
--19th century.
HD8393.H57G78   309.1'41'0810924 [B]   76-8241
ISBN 0-87991-619-2

MANUFACTURED IN THE UNITED STATES OF AMERICA

To Fran

CONTENTS

PREFACE

In the Ford lectures delivered at Oxford in 1960, Professor G. Kitson Clark declared that one major task of Victorian scholarship was that of rescuing the "real men and women who have been shrunk by historians into bloodless units of a generalization."[1] His advice to direct more attention to "those in the shadows in the wings" is one of the reasons for this study. George Jacob Holyoake (1817-1906) was a secondary figure and this work is by no means an attempt to raise him from that status. Holyoake was never elected to Parliament; he never wrote a major book; and he did not even attract a significant number of disciples. He did, as I have discovered, have considerable success in articulating and in helping to form the beliefs and values of one important sector of the Victorian community: the "advanced", as they denoted themselves, sections of the working class. During his long life, Holyoake participated in numerous radical and workingmen's associations: the Owenites, Chartists, cooperators, Secularists and a good many others.

Victorian England was an age of rapid demographic, industrial and social change. Few people have seen the relationships between the component classes of their society so rapidly and yet so peacefully modified. That is not to say that Victorian society was free of tension. As a journalist and self-proclaimed propagandist for the progress of the working classes, Holyoake was compelled to deal with the major concerns of his times. Although his positions were often unpopular he eventually gained respectability for himself and helped to contribute to the comparative social stability which marked the middle years of Victoria's reign. Although this study focuses on the life and work of Holyoake, it has not been my intention to have composed his definitive biography but only to have furnished some insights into the progress of the laboring classes and into those conditions which led so many Victorian people to a sense of assurance about the ability of their social and political institutions to resolve conflicts.

I am indebted to a number of scholars on both sides of the Atlantic but especially to Professors Emmet Larkin of the University of Chicago and John Saville of the University of Hull for their encouragement and criticism. For the shortcomings of this study, I take all responsibility. Mr. Roy Garratt, Librarian at the Cooperative Union in Manchester, was most helpful as was the staff at the Bishopsgate Institute in London. I also wish to thank Moorhead State University for the generous financial support which enabled me to complete my research, and to Mrs. Lou Larson and Ms. Marilyn Jenson for typing the manuscript.

[1] G. Kitson Clark, *The Making of Victorian England* (New York: Atheneum, 1967), p. 13.

CHAPTER I

EARLY YEARS

The Holyoake family had resided in Birmingham for several generations before George Jacob Holyoake was born there on April 13, 1817.[1] Although very little is known of George's paternal grandfather, Jacob Holyoake, he apparently had once operated a small forge in Birmingham until some adversity led him to desert his family. Richard Groves, George's maternal grandfather, was more fortunate as a successful buckle maker; his respectability became well assured when he was appointed a beadle of St. Martin's church. George Jacob's father, George Herbert (1790?-1853), was employed as a mechanic at the Eagle foundry. Because Birmingham industry was characterized at this time by the small shop rather than large factories, the social distance between master and worker was often small and a skilled artisan like George Herbert Holyoake could claim due respect. He was a proud man and independent minded as well, for George Jacob later recalled how his father would refuse to remove his hat in the presence of his master, and how he expressed not the slightest interest in religion.

Catherine Groves Holyoake not only reared eleven children of whom George Jacob was the second, but she also supplemented the family income by manufacturing buttons, a common domestic occupation in the early nineteenth century. Although the Holyoake family was far from being affluent, they were not poverty stricken. Moreover the home at No. 1 Inge Street, described by Holyoake as being "fresh and bright", was located on the still uncongested southern boundary of Birmingham. In none of his later writings did Holyoake ever indicate that his childhood had been unhappy. With the exception that he was a frail boy—he would be subject to illness his entire life—his early years were in no way extraordinary.

At the age of nine, George Jacob proudly began to accompany his father to the Eagle foundry where he soon learned the trade of a whitesmith—finishing, polishing, and working in metal alloys. He

1

also acquired a considerable knowledge of applied mathematics at the foundry but his ability to read and write was gained either at the Wesleyan Sunday School in Carr's Lane, attended at his mother's insistence, or at a "dame's school" which were then quite numerous in Birmingham. By the time he was fourteen, young Holyoake had become adept at his trade and had even contributed a number of minor inventions. For his ingenuity on one occasion, he was awarded a valuable set of mathematical instruments. From 1827 to 1839, Holyoake worked diligently at the foundry and by all appearances he was happy and satisfied in this work. He did observe, however, that sometimes even strong men who lacked his father's skill and self-esteem trembled in their master's presence.

In addition to being a place of employment, the shop was often the scene of considerable political discussion. For example, R.G. Gammage, a contemporary of Holyoake, noted that at this time "there were all sorts of men in the shop, both in politics and religion —Tories, Whigs, and Radicals, Atheists, Deists, Catholics, Church of England men and those who did not profess anything. Amid all the debates that went on in the shop my young ears were always open."[2] Although it cannot be assumed that the Eagle foundry fit this description, it was not unusual for a lad to gain an exposure to politics at a relatively young age. Birmingham had been a principal locus of radical political activity since the end of the Napoleonic wars and it is most improbable that the alert and sensitive young Holyoake took no heed of the journeymen's discussions. Just the opposite appears to be true for Holyoake reports that his interest in political affairs was awakened by the age of fifteen. The issue of the day was, of course, parliamentary reform. "During the active years of the Political Union," he recalled, "my days were spent within a few yards of its office."[3]

In 1829 Thomas Attwood, a Birmingham banker, with the support of two local businessmen, Joshua Scholefield and G.F. Muntz, had begun a campaign to make Westminster more responsive to industrial and commercial interests. When the Prime Minister, the Duke of Wellington, paid no heed to their petitions, Attwood concluded that Parliament itself needed to be reformed. To that end he founded the Political Union for the Protection of Public Rights in order to secure those constitutional changes which would result in a "House of Commons which should reflect the wishes and interests of the mass of intelligent people."[4] Not only did Attwood's Union receive the support of manufacturers but also of large

numbers of independent craftsmen, skilled journeymen and laboring men. Birmingham was a unique city because of the structure of
Birmingham industry. The interests of masters and workmen were
drawn together and the high degree of social mobility tended to blur
class distinctions. Therefore the government's economic policies
were a source of dissatisfaction to nearly everyone.[5]

In 1831 when the Whigs introduced their Reform Bill, the
Birmingham Political Union undertook the mobilization of public
opinion in their support. Monthly meetings were sponsored; sister
unions in neighboring towns were created, and a petition, embodying most of the points which would later appear in the Peoples'
Charter, was sent to Parliament. The demonstrations and platform
orations were a significant feature of young Holyoake's world. What
a spectacle it must have been to him when a crowd estimated at
200,000 met at Newhall Hill on May 7, 1832, to urge the intransigent
Lords to assent to the Reform Bill without alteration "so as not to
drive to despair a high-minded, a generous and fearless people!"[6]
Of the struggle among ministers, parliamentary parties, bishops and
king, Holyoake knew but little. In the first flush of his political
awareness it seemed as if the Reform bill had been a creation of a
massive and persistent agitation. When Attwood and Scholefield
were elected to represent Birmingham in the reformed Commons, all
the city exaulted.

It is a fact that the bill's failure to include the working classes
within the pale of the constitution produced immediate disillusionment—180,000 gathered in Birmingham in May 1833 to protest the
treachery. As E.P. Thompson has demonstrated, that process of
radicalization which would set middle and working classes apart in
Birmingham had already begun.[7] But in the relative prosperity of
the mid-1830s it was difficult to produce organized and massive
protest. For Holyoake, other interests took precedence. Secure in his
employment, he chose to enhance his future prospects by increasing
his formal knowledge. In January 1836 he began attending classes at
the Birmingham Mechanics' Institute.[8]

Organized in 1825, the same year in which Lord Brougham and
Francis Place had founded the first such school in London, the
Birmingham Institute was serving, at this time, over fifteen hundred
members. Both contemporary observers and historians have been
justly skeptical about the benefits obtained by workingmen from
these schools. It is true that the institutes served the ambitious clerk
better than the laboring man who was often too exhausted at the end

of the working day to avail himself of the lectures which frequently were overly advanced for him. The institutes have also been criticized for being carriers of bourgeois values. There is no doubt, however, that the Birmingham Institute, in its relatively short life-span of twenty years, was a fine school with dedicated tutors and a good library. [9]

Holyoake had an excellent tutor at the institute in the person of Daniel Wright, a pioneer of educational programs for workmen in Birmingham. Approaching his studies as avidly as time would allow, Holyoake attended classes in rhetoric, grammar, geometry and trigonometry. He also took advantage of the lectures given by George Combe on phrenology and for a time was very taken by its conclusions regarding man's nature and potential. Evidently Holyoake got on well with his peers for in November 1836 the members of the senior class elected him to be their secretary. [10]

Whatever other ideas he obtained at the institute, none was more important to Holyoake than the conviction that education was a necessary concomitant, and almost a prerequisite, of working class progress. Several years later in one of his first publications, *Practical Grammar* (1844), Holyoake asserted that it is the "despotism of ignorance and incapacity which makes every form of tyranny possible. Intellectual servitude is worse than physical because the physical chain is riveted by others, the mental by ourselves." [11] It is possible to impute much naiveté to such views but they were certainly representative of the great respect for education which accompanied the development of working class consciousness in the early nineteenth century. [12]

When another teacher at the institute, Hawkes Smith, introduced Holyoake to the Unitarians, his educational development took wider scope. His mother was a devout Christian but, like his father, Holyoake had not concerned himself much with such matters. But in the winter of 1836 Holyoake confessed that he had begun to think "seriously of religion." [13] Before this time he held Trinitarian beliefs because a "vague impression existed in my mind that three Gods were not too many to attend to the affairs of this vast universe." [14] His association with the Unitarians encouraged Holyoake to examine the Scriptures thoroughly and he soon became convinced that the doctrines and rituals of Christianity could hardly be accepted by an enlightened person. Although his thinking about Christianity would not fully mature for several more years, Holyoake's movement in the direction of free thought was rapid and unmistakable. By the end of 1837 his infidelity was already well known.[15] His was no isolated experience. The general failure of the church to accommodate to the process of industrialization and urbanization coupled with the hostility shown by the prelates to political reform produced a large number of free thinkers. Their scripture was Paine's *Age of Reason*; their martyrs were men like Richard Carlile who was imprisoned for vending it.

The young sceptic would undoubtedly have continued his career at the foundry had it not been for the resurgence of reform agitation in the late thirties. First as a Chartist, then as a disciple of Robert Owen, Holyoake found himself being drawn even closer to the mainstream of working class radicalism. William Lovett's six-point document, drawn up in the spring of 1838, signalled a new phase in the British working class movement but it certainly was not the beginning of Chartism. It is in such elements as late eighteenth century radicalism, Luddism, the struggle for a free press in the twenties and in disillusionment with the Reform Bill that the origins of Chartism must be located. With the return of unemployment to Birmingham in the late thirties came a demand for the reactivization of the Political Union. This was formally done in the spring of 1837 and Holyoake immediately joined the new political union.[16] In May 1838 the B.P.U. agreed to assist in agitating for the Charter and, for a time, it appeared that cooperation between the Birmingham middle and working classes was once again taking place.[17] But that alliance, weakened severely by the events of 1832, was soon to be destroyed.

On August 6, 1838, Feargus O'Connor, the Irish radical who had broken with Daniel O'Connell several years before, addressed a great Birmingham rally. He chastised the middle class and spoke menacingly of the violence which could be expected if Parliament rejected the Charter. To Attwood and to moderate Chartist leaders like William Lovett, O'Connor was a dangerous and unprincipled man. To be sure he delighted in immoderate rhetoric, but O'Connor did strike responsive chords among the people. More than any other man it was O'Connor who brought national unity to a movement which was so closely tied to local leadership and who contributed to the crystallization of working class consciousness. Soon there was clear division between the middle and working classes. By November 1838 Thomas Attwood was greeted with howls of derision and the revived B.P.U. soon withered.

In June 1839 the Charter, bearing some two million signatures, was presented to Parliament only to be overwhelmingly rejected. As O'Connor had predicted, violence resulted. In July, Holyoake witnessed the disorders which took place in Birmingham's Bull Ring, all the while carefully refraining from active participation. Sporadic outbursts continued, capped by serious rioting in Newport in early November. As a result, over five-hundred Chartist leaders were arrested and either deported or sentenced to short prison terms. Several reasons for Holyoake's hesitancy to become involved in these events may be given. First, his work and studies at the institute allowed him little time for engaging in politics. More important, Holyoake had come to believe that even radical alterations in the constitution would not bring about true progress for the working classes. What first had to be changed was the basic nature of society. This conclusion he had not come to on his own but no doubt he had picked up from the disciples of Robert Owen with whom by 1838 he had become closely associated.

Unlike Chartism, Owenism was never a popular movement. At best, it could claim about 100,000 adherents in its peak years. Yet within Owenite Socialism of the later thirties and early forties are found significant features of British working class consciousness and expectations.[18] The major facets of Owen's career—his success as an industrialist, his conversion of New Lanark into a Scottish manufacturing utopian community, his failure to establish a viable community at New Harmony, Indiana and his attempt to form a national trade union — are all well known. But the real significance of Owenism, and the reason for its powerful attraction even for those who did not formally join a socialist society, was in its projection of a radically different organization of society, a veritable heaven on earth.

It is the industrial revolution itself which provides the context for the study of British socialism. The discussion among historians about the effects of rapid industrial development on a traditionally agrarian society has continued unabated for more than a century. There is no doubt, however, that patterns of behavior and social organization which had existed for generations were greatly disrupted. The discipline of the factory system, the expansion of urban centers and the chaotic nature of early capitalism produced an environment conducive to expectations of great change. A contemporary development was the evangelical revival with its stress on Bible reading and "vital" religion. Together, social disruption and evangelicalism created an environment in which millenarian movements flourished. Prophets arose to predict the second coming of Christ and the thousand year rule of the saints; they found no lack of receptive hearers. Some sects, such as the Shakers, claimed that the millennium had already begun.

Although Owen's eighteenth century rationalism had resulted in 1817 in an explicit condemnation of Christianity for having made men superstitious, bigoted, hypocritical and guilt ridden, his vision of a radically new society was comfortably expressed in millenarian terms. The very first number of the *New Moral World,* for example, stated plainly that

> The rubicon between the Old Immoral and the New Moral Worlds is finally passed. . . . The first coming of Christ was a partial development of Truth to the few, conveyed, of necessity, in dark sayings, parables, and mysteries. The second coming of Christ will make Truth known to the many, and enable all to enjoy the endless benefits in practice which it will insure to mankind. The time is therefore arrived when the foretold millennium is about to commence, when the slave and the prisoner, the bond-man and the bond-woman and the child and the servant, shall be set free for ever, and oppression of body and mind shall be known no more. [19]

Such language was the ideal medium for the dissemination of knowledge about the new moral world. In the increased use of such rhetoric, British socialism was well on the way to becoming a secular millenarian sect.

Owen and his growing number of disciples may also have become more millenarian out of simple frustration. Owen had always held an environmentalist conception of character formation and had therefore made education an integral part of his work both as an industrialist and as a founder of communities. In order to achieve his goal of true society he was forced to conclude that a lengthy period of education would be needed. Neither the time nor the resources existed for the task. The alternative was instant conversion of the working classes to the values of the new society and the immediate establishment of communities based upon those values. Thus two polarities came to exist within Owenism: the one position still envisioned progress and a new world won through education and the other was anxious to commence the millennium Owenites argued among themselves over many issues but no question was more vital than this. A few of Owen's disciples became so thoroughly millenarian—John Finch was one—that they really did conceive of Owen as the second messiah. In October 1839 when the Owenites purchased 533 acres of land in Hampshire in order to build the community of Queenwood, the more ardent millennialists were especially gratified. But the majority of Owen's followers, especially those young men of the mechanics' institutes, combined their hope for a new society with the continuing belief in the importance of education.

It was the integral role of education in bringing about social change which had undoubtedly attracted Holyoake to Owenism. Hawkes Smith was prominent in Birmingham Owenism and Holyoake's closest friend at the institute, Frederick Hollick, had become an Owenite social missionary. Holyoake had first heard Owen speak in June 1836 and in February 1838 he joined Owen's Association of All Classes of All Nations. (In May 1839 partly to protect their funds under the law and partly as the result of Owenism's increasingly sectarian character, the Owenites incorporated their two official bodies—the National Community Friendly Society and the Association of All Classes of All Nations—into the Universal Community Society of Rational Religionists. Executive power lay in the hands of the Central Board of the U.C.S.R.R.).

Although Chartists and Socialists had different objectives, it must not be supposed that the two movements were at complete odds or had nothing to do with each other. Both were expressions of general working class discontent and many men, like Holyoake, were involved in both organizations. The Owenites were not hostile to political reform but they did generally follow the direction of Owen, a political conservative, who had concluded that the Charter could be won only through violence and revolution. Of such he had utter horror.[20]   More important, the Owenites were convinced that political reform would in no way alter the inequities of their society. Rather than continuing to pursue the "obstacle-encumbered path to universal suffrage," the Chartists were encouraged to "unite with the socialists. . . This is the shortest, easiest and best way to secure 'equal rights' to all." [21] It must also be considered that the Chartists, although they were by no means antipathetic to education, had not made it an integral feature of their program. For many young workers, such as Holyoake, education was of utmost importance; they found their sympathies therefore quite naturally swinging to Owenism.

The violence which followed the rejection of the Charter confirmed the Owenites in their beliefs. Henry Jeffrey, social missionary in Edinburgh, expressed the opinion generally accepted by Owenites when he wrote in the *New Moral World* that "every honest man, especially every Socialist, must regard the recent Birmingham riot as a wanton and cowardly attack upon property, as a foolish attempt to destroy, caring not what . . .In the *New Moral World* they have continually been told that their Charter will not remove the evils under which they labour because those evils are more the result of social than political error."[22] With the leading Chartists in custody, the Chartist presses destroyed and with the movement in temporary disarray the Owenite position seemed all the more reasonable. To the Owenites' credit, the *New Moral World* did not disparage Chartism in the hour of its first defeat. Hawkes Smith even claimed that, while the Owenites held "themselves aloof from political agitation," they did consider themselves to be Chartists "in the abstract." Political reform would be more easily and naturally secured, continued Smith, when the working class had first achieved the "means of a good sound, practical education, and of permanent, profitable beneficial leisure affording employment."[23]

This critique of Chartism, presented by men for whom Holyoake had utmost respect, made considerable sense to him. Perhaps he had already considered throwing in his lot more actively with the Owenties. Circumstances soon pushed him in that direction. After the July disorders Birmingham was once again in a state of comparative tranquility. Work at the foundry was slow and Holyoake, now married, was continuing his studies at the institute.[24] In early September, Daniel Wright suddenly died. The students at the institute immediately informed the directors that, in their opinion, "there is no individual so well qualified as Mr. G.J. Holyoake to succeed our revered and much lamented tutor."[25] This position carried with it considerable prestige and Holyoake undoubtedly believed himself a likely appointee because he had served as Wright's assistant and had also held other minor posts at the institute. In the expectation of receiving that assignment, he quit his job. He was soon informed, however, that he would not receive the position; the following January, he resigned from the institute.

Little mystery lies behind this course of events. The directors had refused him the position because of his religious and social unorthodoxy. Manufacturers who supervised the institutes desired only that their employees be instructed in practical knowledge;

heterodox political opinions and especially ideas subversive to the Christian religion were not to be allowed.[26] His well known association with the Owenites and his disavowal of Christianity blocked his appointment. Although there is no record that teachers such as Hawkes Smith who had become Owenites were dismissed, the directors were not about to place other Owenites in those positions.

Upon hearing of Holyoake's plight, Frederick Hollick, serving the Owenites in Sheffield, encouraged Holyoake to apply for a post similar to his own.

> Why the devil don't you turn Social Missionary, eh? Don't say you can't. I know you *can*. You know what you would have to teach and expound, and you are aware that your previous studies have so habituated you to return to *first principles* (undoubtedly a reference to Holyoake's training in mathematics), and that is all you have to do in 'Social Lecturing'.[27]

This advice was taken seriously. After he resigned from the institute, Holyoake managed by private tutoring to make a meagre living for Eleanor and himself. But when their first child, Madeline, was born in May 1840, Holyoake's responsibilities increased. The weekly wage of a social missionary was thirty shillings, not an insubstantial sum. He therefore made the decision to follow Hollick's suggestion. Hollick recommended Holyoake's name to the Central Board, and he also received the endorsement of the Birmingham socialists.[28]

Because their funds were limited and because Holyoake's name was quite probably unfamiliar to them, the Central Board made no haste to come to a decision. Another alternative, however, was available to Holyoake. In addition to social missionaries who received their salary from the Central Board, it was possible to become assigned as a stationed lecturer. The duties were comparable—lecturing and organizing—but the stationed lecturers received compensation directly from the socialist branch which they served. This feature made the lecturer's financial position more precarious because the local societies invariably had difficulties with funds.

Because their branch was small the Owenites of Worcester, only twenty-six miles from Birmingham, were ineligible to receive the regular services of a social missionary. The Central Board suggested that Holyoake might serve them as a stationed lecturer. Contact was made and Holyoake set out from Birmingham on foot, arriving in Worcester on August 21, 1840. One week later, he delivered his first lectures: "An Enquiry into the Incentives offered by present Society to the practice of Honour, Honesty, and Virtue" and "General Intelligence, the only agent necessary for the Diffusion of the Rational Religion." The Worcester socialists were extremely pleased with the performances, informing the readers of the *New Moral World* that Holyoake had greatly impressed them with his "pleasing manner of lecturing, the depth of knowledge and extensive reading." [29]

Holyoake was offered the position; he accepted; and the Worcester Branch asked the Central Board to ratify the agreement. In September, the Board complied with the request. [30]

NOTES TO CHAPTER ONE

[1] Major facts of Holyoake's early life are recounted in his autobiography, *Sixty Years of an Agitator's Life* (London: T.Fisher Unwin, 1892), I, 7-25. See also Joseph McCabe *Life and Letters of George Jacob Holyoake* (London: Watts and Co., 1908), I, 1-36. See also E. Royle, "George Jacob Holyoake," *Dictionary of Labour Biography*. Joyce M. Bellamy and John Saville, eds. (London: Macmillan, 1972), I, pp. 182-189.

[2] R.G. Gammage, *History of the Chartist Movement* (New York: Augustus M. Kelley Publishers, 1969), p. 6. This reference is found in the introduction by John Saville.

[3] Holyoake, *Sixty Years*, I, 25.

[4] Conrad Gill, *History of Birmingham* (London: Oxford University Press, 1952), p. 205.

[5] See especially Asa Briggs, "Social Structure and Politics in Birmingham and Lyons (1825-1848)," *British Journal of Sociology*, I (March, 1950), 67-80 and Asa Briggs, "The Background to the Parliamentary Reform Movement in Three English Cities (1830-1832)," *Cambridge Historical Journal*, X (1952), 293-317.

[6] Gill, *History of Birmingham*, p. 209.

[7] E.P. Thompson, *The Making of the English Working Class* (New York: Vintage Books, 1963), pp. 826-27.

[8] G.J. Holyoake, *Log Book No. 1* (March 31, 1836), Holyoake Collection, Bishopsgate Institute, London [Hereafter noted as B.I.].

[9] For general material on the nature of the mechanics' institutes see especially Mabel Tylecote, *The Mechanics' Institutes of Lancashire and Yorkshire Before 1851* (Manchester: The University Press, 1957) and J.F.C. Harrison, *Learning and Living, 1790-1960* (Toronto: The University of Toronto Press, 1961). Although there is no specific study of the Birmingham Mechanics' Institute, see the very relevant information in Edward Royle, "Mechanics' Institutes and the Working Classes, 1840-1860," *The Historical Journal*, XIV (1971) 318-320.

[10] Holyoake, *Log Book No. 1* (November 27, 1836), B.I.

[11] G.J. Holyoake, *Practical Grammer* (London: Watson, 1844), p. 7.

[12] This conclusion is drawn with great clarity by E.P. Thompson, *The Making of the English Working Class*, pp. 711-19, 732-46.

[13] Holyoake, *Log Book No. 1* (February 8, 1836), B.I.

[14] Holyoake, *Sixty Years*, I, 35.

[15] Holyoake, *Log Book No. 1* (January 9, 1838), B.I.

[16] *Ibid.* (April, 1837), B.I.

[17] For the development of Chartism in Birmingham see especially Asa Briggs (ed.), *Chartist Studies* (London: Macmillan, 1959), pp. 1-28 and E.P. Thompson, *The Making of the English Working Class*, pp. 826-28.

[18] The bicentenary of Owen's birth has produced a flurry of scholarship. See the fine essays in Sidney Pollard and John Salt (eds.), *Robert Owen: Prophet of the Poor* (London: MacMillan Press, Ltd., 1971). By far the most significant study of Owenism is J.F.C. Harrison, *Quest for the New Moral World* (New York: Charles Scribner's Sons, 1969). Frank Podmore, *Robert Owen* (New York: D. Appleton and Company, 1907) is a book still worthy of consideration. See also W.H.G. Armytage,

Heavens Below (Toronto: University of Toronto Press, 1961), pp. 77-167.

19 *New Moral World*, I, No. 1 (November 1, 1834), 1.

20 Robert Owen's political conservatism has been the subject of serious consideration. See Ralph Miliband, "The Politics of Robert Owen," *Journal of the History of Ideas*, XV (April, 1954), 233-245.

21 *New Moral World*, V, No. 19 (March 2, 1839), 296.

22 *Ibid.*, VI, No. 43 (August 17, 1839), 686-87.

23 *Ibid.*, No. 42 (August 10, 1839), 671.

24 Holyoake indicated that he made the acquaintance of his wife in a Unitarian bookshop. After a short courtship, he and Eleanor Williams were married in a civil ceremony on March 10, 1839.

25 *Letterbook*, (September 14, 1839), B.I.

26 Tylecote, *The Mechanics' Institutes*, p. 110 and Harrison, *Learning and Living*, p. 83.

27 Hollick to Holyoake, *Letterbook* (January 19, 1840), B.I.

28 Hollick to Holyoake, *Letterbook* (May 16, 1840), B.I. and Birmingham District Board to Walter Newall, Secretary of Central Board (July 22, 1840), No. 15, Holyoake Collection, Cooperative Union, Ltd., Manchester [hereafter noted as C.U.].

29 *New Moral World*, VIII, No. 11 (September 12, 1840), 172.

30 Holyoake, *Log Book No. 1* (September, 1840), B.I.

CHAPTER II

A CRITIC OF OWEN

Although the twenty-three year old lecturer was thoroughly committed to Owenism, it is doubtful that Holyoake fully shared its communitarian aspirations. He embarked on his new career with great enthusiasm, believing that his work was contributing significantly to social regeneration. He had learned to expect that the new world would be one in which the working classes would receive the total fruit of satisfying labor. The new society would be founded on reason, not superstition, and the pleasures of the flesh would be replaced by those of the intellect. Such ideas were the soul of Owenism but were not the special property of those who could foresee the new moral world only in terms of community building.

In many ways Holyoake was equal to his tasks; he certainly thought so. He was intelligent, he had inherited the inveterate optimism of his teachers regarding the potential for achieving progress through education, and he was willing to work to the limits of his energy. He could not fail because he did not expect to fail. And if for some reason the work did not prove to be successful, the fault would not be his.

At first, all went very well. The fact that Eleanor and Madeline had to remain in Birmingham until December—he commuted frequently—was of no serious bother to him. Immediately he was elected president of the society. By his own estimate, the Worcester Socialists prospered. On November 4, the third anniversary of the branch was celebrated by a public dinner and a ball which "went off with unusual éclat." [1] His initial enthusiasm was soon tempered, however, because of an obvious lack of interest in his lectures. In December he sourly confessed that there was "no appreciation of intellect here." [2] Although his knowledge and wit had provided instruction and amusement for his small audiences, Holyoake was not a commanding figure on the lecture platform. He had neither the strong voice to be an orator nor the flamboyancy to demand continuing attention.

15

Another unpleasantness was debt. Holyoake detested being in the position of owing other men but the previous June he had borrowed £17 from a T.A. Jackson to help his parents set up a small business.³ This sum had to be repaid and still he had to support his family on a stipend of less tha: thirty shillings a week. Once again he was forced to turn to private tutoring. Although the winter of 1841 was not by any means pleasant for him, Holyoake did further his education in socialism by plunging into William Thompson's massive *Inquiry into the Principles of the Distribution of Wealth Most Conducive to Human Happiness.*⁴

Two significant and related developments took place during Holyoake's assignment in Worcester. First, a more cordial relationship was established between the Chartists and the Owenites. The Chartists had sought to obtain a hall for a New Year's Eve benefit ball for Chartist leaders in prison. They first went to Worcester churches and, when refused those facilities, turned to the Socialists. Holyoake made the Hall of Science available. As a consequence, a "friendly" feeling was established between the two groups and in May 1841 they jointly sponsored a public discussion on the subject of which one of the two organizations could bring the greatest benefits to the working classes.⁵

Not everyone in Worcester was delighted to witness this apparent bond between Chartists and Socialists. The editor of the *Worcester Herald* deplored it, accusing the Chartists of a further sin by mixing their radicalism with the immorality of the Socialists. Certainly this charge of immorality had absolutely no foundation. In his writings, especially in the *Book of the New Moral World*, Owen had asserted that the unbreakable marriage contract should be abolished and that child-rearing should become a function of the community. These instructions, taken completely out of context, were interpreted to mean that unlimited liasons, together with the illegitimate offspring, would be on the agenda of the new moral world. A typical bit of invective was that offered by Rev. Joseph Barker, a New Connexion minister. After accusing the Socialists of planning to overthrow all accepted social institutions and to do away with religion, he also condemned them for desiring "to live and herd together like beasts of the field."⁶

In Worcester, a Reverend Wake began to preach against the Socialists and when Holyoake visited Cheltenham in late January 1841 he found the Reverend John Brindley condemning Socialist infidelity and immorality. Holyoake responded by writing letters to both the *Worcester Herald* and to the *Worcester Chronicle* denouncing the editors for allowing such libel to be reprinted in their papers.[7] Quite correctly Holyoake sensed that such charges, no matter how false, could be detrimental to the growth of Socialism. His anti-clerical attitude, always a part of his infidelity, was greatly increased by these clerical denunciations of Socialism. Holyoake was now convinced that the Owenites must make the combating of religion and clergy one of their highest priorities.

Although he was secretly dissatisfied with the Worcester situation, Holyoak's efforts had attracted favorable attention. At the 1841 Congress of the UCSRR, the decision was made to transfer Holyoake to the larger Sheffield Branch.[8] At first, he was again filled with enthusiasm. "I like it," he wrote to Eleanor on May 18, "and what is of more importance, both to you and me, the people like me."[9] In addition to lecturing, Holyoake established and conducted a day school in Sheffield. For his labor, he received thirty shillings a week from the society. Although this was not an insubstantial sum, it was five shillings less than the rate established by the Central Board for married men with less than three children.

But once again his initial enthusiasm soon waned. "Neither my School nor my lectures well attended," he recorded in June. "Weary of my employment. But for Jackson, I would resign it." In July he confided, "my enthusiasm sinking to zero."[10] By the autumn, however, his spirits had risen a bit. There were fifty pupils in the school and he was able to appoint an assistant, Thomas Paterson, to carry on the instruction when he was delivering an occasional lecture elsewhere.

The reasons for Holyoake's disillusionment are not difficult to discover. First, the Sheffield Branch was experiencing financial difficulty, as were most other societies. They owed £300 on their hall. The Central Board was continually asking for money, and the general depression of the 1840s was already being reflected in the society's declining revenues. Secondly, the Central Board was not enthusiastic about Socialist day schools. Some opposition had been voiced against them at the annual congress in May and in July, Walter Newall made the Board's position on the matter emphatically clear to Holyoake.

> Regarding schools the Board would be sorry to damp the energy of any of our members but the most we can accomplish at present will be to keep the children as much as possible from vicious

associations, to give them habits of order and
cleanliness, and to answer their enquiries respect-
ing themselves and the things by which they are
immediately surrounded; this accompanied by
attention to their small personal wants, and taking
care their place of meeting us be properly venti-
lated at all times. [11]

This attitude may not have been representative of Owenite opinion
regarding the education of children, but Holyoake must have been
nonetheless discouraged to receive it.

Finally, it did not appear that the Central Board was
sufficiently aware of the importance of responding to clerical attacks
delivered from the pulpit and in the press. While it is true that
Christians had been hostile to Owen ever since his famous
denunciation of religion in 1817, it was only when Socialism
assumed a more sectarian character that both established and
dissenting clergy had begun a systematic attack. Many clergymen
had the seriousness of Socialism brought to their attention by Henry
Phillpotts, the pugnacious, ultra-conservative Bishop of Exeter.
Phillpotts despised Lord Melbourne. When Melbourne granted
Owen an audience with Queen Victoria in June 1839, he was
criticized in the press. Phillpotts saw an opportunity to discredit
both Melbourne and the Socialists at the same time.

On January 24, 1840, he presented a petition to the House of
Lords signed by numerous clergymen, magistrates and merchants of
Birmingham complaining that the morality of the people was being
corrupted by a "system called Socialism."[12]   There were, he
reported, sixty Socialist ·societies and dozens of missionaries who
regularly visited over three hundred towns to distribute their
immoral literature. This organization, Phillpotts contended, was not
only illegal but treasonable as well. Demanding that the government
take action, especially against the circulation of "blasphemous and
immoral" publications, Phillpotts concluded his attack by quoting
an astute observation made in the *Westminster Review:* "Owenism in
one form or another, is at present the actual creed of a great portion
of the working classes."[13] Although Phillpotts' harangue made
little impression on the Peers, many local magistrates and clergy
were aroused. There were laws prohibiting blasphemy and they
could perhaps be applied to the Owenites.

Persecution often strengthens group solidarity. Upon the
Socialists, however, it seems to have had the opposite effect. The

one-time advocate of free thought now counseled his social ✓ missionaries to speak sympathetically of religion. "Let your hearers," he advised them in 1839, "compare your truth with their old prejudices." Lecturers were instructed to avoid arguments by "kindly and respectfully" declining to hold discussion of religious questions.[14] At all costs Owen wished to avoid unnecessary controversy which would endanger the success of his communal projects. In keeping with Owen's directive, the editor of the *New Moral World,* G.A. Fleming, urged the social missionaries to go so far as to make public confessions of orthodox Protestantism if requested to ✓ do so. No policy could have been more repugnant to those who had rejoiced at Owen's earlier statements about religion and who believed that the church and clergy of all denominations were the greatest obstacles to political and social progress. Charles Southwell, former missionary in London, speaking in opposition to Lloyd Jones, a prominent social missionary who had no objection to Owen's new policy, proclaimed at the 1841 Congress that he would rather fall dead on the platform than to make such a confession.[15] Henry Jeffrey of Edinburgh, Frederick Hollick and Holyoake were also convinced that the profession of religious orthodoxy would lead to ✓ the destruction of the new moral world. They equated deference with submission and vowed to speak their minds freely in matters of religion.

In November 1841 Southwell, with the aid of William Chilton, a Bristol printer, and Malthus Ryall, a London engraver, began to publish the *Oracle of Reason* to refute the passive position being taken by the *New Moral World* on the religious question. Southwell's opening editorial claimed that the *Oracle* would "deal out Atheism as freely as ever Christianity was dealt out to the people." Doubting "whether such a paper will be permitted by the authorities of this country," Southwell foresaw and indeed welcomed "consequences of a serious nature" for those involved.[16] Southwell deliberately began his publication on a provocative note by devoting each of the early numbers to articles refuting the existence of God and discussing the evidence for the transformation of the species, a ✓ much debated subject long before Charles Darwin's publications. It is unclear what Holyoake's contribution was to the first efforts of this little group of radicals. Although he later referred to himself as part of a "Defiant Syndicate of Four" (Southwell, Chilton, Ryall, and Holyoake), the documents indicate that Chilton and Ryall did not make his acquaintance until after the *Oracle* had begun to

appear.[17] Furthermore, no articles in the *Oracle* were initialed by
Holyoake until after the beginning of 1842.

With the fourth number of the *Oracle*, Southwell drew the
reaction which he had predicted. He ridiculed the Bible or "Jew
Book" as a "revoltingly, odious Jew Production, a history of lust,
sodomies, wholesale slaughtering, and horrible depravity."[18] Hardly had the issue reached the shops when Southwell was arrested on a
charge of blasphemy. When he was brought to trial on January 14,
1842, Southwell presented a lengthy defense appealing to the right of
free speech. Neither personal beliefs nor their expression, he
asserted, were proper subjects for social judgement. He was,
however, duly convicted of "impious, blasphemous, and profane
libel of and concerning the Holy Scriptures and Religion," sentenced
to be imprisoned for one year and fined £ 100.[19]

The actions of Southwell might have been dismissed by the
Central Board as pure cavil if the religious issue had been his only
concern. Before being interned, however, Southwell had begun to
publish a series of open letters to the Socialists. After announcing his
resignation as a social missionary, Southwell summarized precisely
the dissatisfaction which not only the "defiant syndicate" but also
many rank and file Owenites were beginning to experience:

> The pure philosophy once taught by Robert Owen
> is the very poetry of politics. Now the pure ore is all
> but lost amid the dross and rubbish by which it is
> encumbered. . .Those who called Socialism 'moral
> Chartism' caught the true idea of what Socialism
> was. [20]

Southwell confessed that his own inspiration had initially come from
Owen. As recently as 1840 he had written a short, popular exposition
of Owen's philosophy in which he stated that "the evils of society lie
deep; Mr. Owen has probed them to their source, which source is
competition."[21] Now, Southwell had only words of condemnation
for Owen:

> My judgement condemns the abandonment of
> principle of which the Social representatives have
> been guilty; my judgement heartily despises the
> hesitating, shuffling, equivocating, white feather
> policy that has been pursued for some time past,
> but more especially since the period when the

Bishop of Exeter attacked you in the House of
Lords.[22]

Although the *New Moral World* declared Southwell's arrest to be
most unfortunate, it cannot be said that it deplored the actions of
the authorities.[23] Southwell was spreading dissension. His imprisonment, therefore, removed a thorn from the Socialist body and,
at the same time, it vindicated the position that assaults on
Christianity brought no beneficial results.

Charles Southwell certainly was a man who delighted in making
great issues out of the most insignificant grievances. In this instance,
however, he had accurately defined a problem which would grow for
the Owenites. By no longer insisting upon a complete spiritual
conversion they had begun to surrender a major weapon of their
ideological arsenal. Soon the major concern of the Owenite
leadership would be the survival of the Queenwood colony and even
this task was to become too great.

During the time that Southwell was in the process of getting
himself arrested, Holyoake continued to perform his duties in
Sheffield. On November 28, 1841, he delivered a lecture on trade
union policy to which the Sheffield unionists had been invited. He
pointed out the service rendered by the unions in resisting
oppression, but went on to question their usefulness in times of
technological unemployment or glutted markets. Union treasuries,
he said, were wasted on strikes when they could better be used to
purchase land for the establishment of productive communities. ✓
This lecture, which became Holyoake's first publication a few weeks
later, illustrates that he still acknowledged the validity of Owen's
communal plans. Holyoake did, however, append a paragraph to
this published lecture in which he criticized those who pay court to
wealth at the expense of honesty.[24]

It probably came as a surprise to Holyoake when, in December
1841, he received a letter from William Chilton asking him to
become the nominal editor of the *Oracle of Reason*. "There must, I
imagine, be a name attached to the *Oracle*," Chilton pointed out, "I
am not a coward but within these twelve hours it has occurred to me
that a post of danger would be injurious to our plans."[25] Chilton
would apparently continue as the real editor although Holyoake,
who accepted the offer, would take the risk of being arrested if the
Oracle offended again. Early in January, Malthus Ryall, who was in
London trying to gather funds for Southwell's defense, promised

Holyoake the same support which he had given the *Oracle* under Southwell.[26]

The *Oracle* continued for a short time to be published regularly under Southwell's name, but Holyoake's name appeared on the masthead of the eighth number, February 12, 1842. His first leader—an attempt at sophistication in which he drew liberally from Shelley, Bentham, Milton, Addison and the Greeks—vowed that the *Oracle* would be continued on Southwell's principles.[27] Uncraftsmanlike though it was, Holyoake's editorial pleased Southwell very much.[28] The tone of the *Oracle*, however, immediately became less belligerent. Holyoake provoked no righteous indignation by writing that most men seemed to be concerned, not with God, but with science and the material world. It was neither blasphemous to cite examples of the discrepancy between the Christians' utterances about peace and love and the persecution and bigotry which they practiced, nor could anyone realistically take exception to Holyoake's remarks that the poor would soon starve if they had only revelation to sustain them, while the wealthy found gospels and good dinners to be an ideal combination. If the poor were interested in social progress, he continued, they would do well to follow the lead of atheists because atheists did not allow themselves to be deluded by Christian exhortations to obedience and piety.[29] His first efforts, unpolished as they were, reveal Holyoake's potential to become a successful working class journalist. He avoided those complicated and metaphysical arguments which were the ruin of so many attempts to enlighten the lower classes. Holyoake also abandoned sensationalism, which might attract a few readers but probably frightened more, for a style which was light, witty, and generally appealing to an unphilosophical public.

During these months in which he was editing the *Oracle*, Holyoake was also refining his own religious views. He always had been something of a Deist; at least he was willing to acknowledge that some external force seemed to be operative in the universe. After Southwell's arrest, Holyoake reconsidered his position. A God who presumed to be omniscient and merciful and yet allowed such evil in his creation must either be a monster or not omnipotent. By April 1842, Holyoake had adopted the classic atheist position that the existence of misery and pain is proof positive that there is no God."[30] When this statement was questioned by one of the *Oracle's* readers, Holyoake assumed a slightly different theological stance, one that he would retain all his life and from which he could never be shaken. "I as an atheist simply profess that I do not see sufficient reason to believe that there is a god. I do not pretend to know that there is no god."[31]   Because the term "agnostic" had yet to be coined, Holyoake continued, until he chose to call himself a "Secularist," to refer to himself as an atheist.

The indifference of the Socialists to Southwell's persecution was a grievance Holyoake could not ignore. How could sure progress be made until Owenism had reasserted its rejection of religion and had presented a firm stand against the oppression of the Christians? Hoping to convince his fellow field workers that they must assume the initiative, Holyoake canvassed the social missionaries as to the feasibility of conducting "anti-superstition" classes. H.Jeffrey of Edinburgh, who was sympathetic to Holyoake's concerns and who recognized the basic irreconcilability between the Christian and Owenite view of human nature, was not optimistic. He related that whenever his Scottish audiences heard anything said against religion, it "nearly frightened them from their seats" because they had become accustomed to associate socialism with practical or primitive Christianity. Precious effort and unnecessary time, thought Jeffrey, would be wasted on this scheme when a more serious issue was at stake. If Holyoake were a true Socialist, he would be trying to turn the society more toward reaching the working classes. The real danger, counseled Jeffrey, was that the Socialists were losing sight of their ultimate goal—the radical reconstruction of social institutions—as they tried to establish a community. If this happened, they would become a mere sect like the Shakers or Rappites.[32]   Jeffrey's opinion that Owenism was becoming little more than an attempt to build a communal farm in Hampshire was persuasive. Nothing more was heard from Holyoake on the subject of anti-superstition classes, but he nevertheless continued to chastise the Central Board for its failure to defend Southwell.

The Board's response to Holyoake's charges was not quite the same as it had been to those of Southwell. They were, no doubt, well aware of Holyoake's exertions, popularity and success in Worcester and Sheffield. The General Secretary, William Galpin, in reference to Holyoake's tract on trade unions, politely assured him that Owen had never sacrificed principle to expediency. While all Socialists had complete freedom to express criticism, Holyoake should realize that unity would not be achieved without agreement as to goals and their means of attainment. As for Southwell, wrote Galpin, no organization could be bound to defend the particular actions of each and every member.[33]   Galpin did his best to avoid a journalistic conflict involving personalities. Even Owen's closest associates and admirers were aware that he was becoming dogmatic and therefore particularly vulnerable to criticism.

On March 22, 1842, Galpin notified Holyoake and all other missionaries that, by decision of the Central Board, their positions would have to be renewed every three months.[34]   Unless the annual congress, to be held in May, renewed it, Holyoake's position in Sheffield would terminate automatically three months later. Funds were becoming very scarce and every available shilling was being mobilized for the community in Hampshire. Before the end of 1842, all missionaries were released because they could no longer be paid. Holyoake, however, had quit his position almost immediately after receiving the notice from Galpin—a decision which initiated an extraordinary series of events.

Holyoake had found Sheffield an increasingly unrewarding station. Because the society could afford but one lecture a week, Holyoake's salary was reduced. In early May, therefore, he moved his family back to Birmingham and from there he set out on foot toward Bristol where, he had heard, there might be a better opportunity for a young Socialist lecturer to earn his living. On the way, he stopped to deliver a lecture in Cheltenham. Approximately one hundred Socialists and Chartists gathered on the evening of May 24 to hear Holyoake deliver a standard talk entitled "Home Colonization as a Means of Superseding Poor-Laws and Emigration." At the conclusion of the lecture, time was alloted for questions. One person present asked if chapels were to be erected in these colonies.[35]   These communities, Holyoake replied rather jovially, would be too poor to build churches. "I appeal to your heads and your pockets if we are not too poor to have a god. If poor men cost the state as much, they would be put, like officers, upon half pay. I think that while our distress lasts, it would be wise to do the same thing with the deity." When the audience had stopped laughing, Holyoake continued more seriously: "I am not religious— my creed is to have no religion. While Southwell is in jail, I flee the bible as a viper, I wish not to hear the name of God and revolt at the touch of a Christian."[36]   After these comments, the meeting adjourned and, the next day, Holyoake continued on his way.

Shortly after his arrival in Bristol, Holyoake received news that the *Cheltenham Chronicle* was calling his remarks blasphemous and criticizing the superintendent of police for not bringing Holyoake to justice. Very likely nothing further would have developed had not Holyoake felt it absolutely necessary to return to Cheltenham, face his accusers and defend his right to express his opinions freely in matters of religion. He set out immediately for Cheltenham. There, on June 2, he delivered a well-advertised address to a group of Chartists at the Cheltenham Mechanics' Institute. During the meeting, the police arrived, and after allowing Holyoake to finish his lecture, they arrested him. The following day, Holyoake was removed to Gloucester prison where he remained until June 17, when bail was finally arranged by some of his friends in Worcester. His trial was scheduled for August 15 at the Gloucester assizes.

Holyoake's arrest was one more justification of the position to which the Central Board adhered. William Galpin, who had been on good terms with Holyoake, now expressed the view that his arrest actually benefited the Socialists because it removed one whose only virtue was "in excitement and haranguing of opponents."[37]   A number of Socialists did offer financial aid to Holyoake. Thomas Paterson began to collect funds for Holyoake's defense, but he received a less than enthusiastic response. Socialist branches in Glasgow and Edinburgh indicated that their members were sympathetic but too hard pressed for money already. At Manchester, Stockport and Macclesfield, Socialists and Chartists held meetings to demonstrate their support for Holyoake.[38]

Between the release and trial, Holyoake spent most of his time in London justifying his actions and seeking support. He could not, he wrote in the *Oracle*, have remained silent in Cheltenham. Never did he purposely seek the role of a martyr, but for doing what seemed his duty, Holyoake was willing to accept the consequences.[39] When a Cheltenham bookseller and his wife, George and Harriet Adams, were arrested in July for selling the *Oracle*, Holyoake's behavior appeared to have been more reasonable than the Socialists had at first been willing to admit. To what length might this persecution go? Holyoake, of course, defended the Adamses in the *Oracle*, taking this opportunity to condemn the increase of intolerance and to chide the Socialists and free-thinkers for not rising to the defense of the persecuted.[40]   He did, however, emphasize that he was still proud to be a Socialist even though he had expected to be dismissed from the organization. Holyoake also declared that, even though he was its editor, he did not approve of all which appeared in the *Oracle of Reason*.[41]   Quite probably he was referring to the articles of Southwell which Holyoake was obliged to print and which, while being very critical of the Socialists, were not constructive.

As the date of his trial drew closer, the support for Holyoake increased. Malthus Ryall had created an Anti-Prosecution Union (a short time later the organization became the Anti-Persecution Union) for the purpose of raising money; the Chartists in Sheffield and the large Socialist branch in London were collecting funds. In Parliament, J.A. Roebuck questioned the Home Secretary about Holyoake's "improper commital." [42]　Even William Galpin wrote him a friendly letter, replete with advice but devoid this time of condemnation. [43]　Holyoake was especially gratified when Richard Carlile, imprisoned in the 1820's for publishing the works of Tom Paine, sought him out and promised to stand by him at his forthcoming trial. For the moment, Holyoake could enjoy his popularity.

In August Holyoake left London, stopped in Birmingham to see his family and then proceeded to Gloucester. On August 15, 1842, he met his peers. A plea of not guilty to the charge of blasphemy was registered although Holyoake admitted that he had spoken in jest of God. He conducted his own defense—a long nine-hour summary of free thought concluded by a discourse on the common law. Carlile thought Holyoake's self-defense was very persuasive indeed; "the most splendid of the kind ever delivered in this country. . . I could scarcely restrain myself from jumping into the dock to embrace you on several occasions." [44]　The wearied jury—seven farmers, a grocer, poulterer, maltster, miller, and shop-keeper—spent however only ten minutes in reaching its verdict. Holyoake was found guilty of the charge and was sentenced to remain in the Gloucester jail for six months. [45]　Thomas Paterson now assumed the nominal editorship of the *Oracle of Reason* and Holyoake immediately began to serve his sentence.

*****

Six months' confinement did not pass easily for him. Never physically robust, Holyoake found the prison diet and lack of exercise very disagreeable. Few visitors were permitted him and Holyoake's communication with the *Oracle* was infrequent. [46]　More irritating to Holyoake than various deprivations were the efforts of warden and chaplain to convert him to Christianity; it was even hinted that a reprieve might be his should he make his confession. Worst of all, in mid-October, Holyoake was notified that his two year old daughter, Madeline, suffering from a "fever" complicated by malnutrition, had died. Holyoake seldom refers to family affairs in his autobiographic writings. He traveled constantly and changed plans too often to have been much engaged in family life, but it is incorrect to assume that he cared but little for his wife and children. The death of his first child under such circumstances surely must have caused him to reflect on his own role as a martyr for he well knew that he could have provided an adequate living if he had not involved himself with the Owenites.

Such suffering might have caused Holyoake to sink into a state of melancholy and apathy. But it did not. Instead he threw himself into writing. The first piece, entitled *A Short and Easy Method with the Saints*, was a condemnation of Christian bigotry, persecution and hypocrisy. "Christians can rob infidels of liberty," he confidently concluded, "but not of honour. . ."[47] The second effort was more ambitious. In hopes of converting Holyoake, a local clergyman had presented him with a copy of William Paley's *Natural Theology* (1802). In order to infer the existence of God, Paley had again relied on the argument that a designed universe made such a conclusion reasonable. In his *Paley Refuted in His Own Words*, Holyoake presented a rather standard materialistic critique of natural theology.[48] It simply was not possible, he argued, to infer the supernatural from actual experience. Secondly, if God himself is intelligent, then he too must have had a creator. Although the book eventually went through six editions, it was a dull and stale attack on a type of theological argument which was already becoming passé. Holyoake was no imaginative theoretician; at best he could adequately summarize the arguments of others. As his *Short and Easy Method with the Saints* revealed, Holyoake's strength was as a persistent critic, a man who could portray in starkest terms the values which men claim to possess and the deeds which they actually perform.

Upon his release on February 6, 1843, Holyoake found himself in demand on the lecture circuit, not as a preacher of Socialism, but as the "Liberated Blasphemer." For several months, he traveled about and when interest in tales of his trial and prison experiences waned, he finally settled for a short time in Worcester. In May 1843 Holyoake traveled to London, arriving completely penniless. There, Branch "53" of the Rational Society (the Socialists had shortened

UCSRR to the Rational Society) offered Holyoake the post of secretary at the wage of ten shillings per week.[49]   It was very little money, but Holyoake accepted hoping again to increase his income by lecturing and tutoring.

Holyoake did not resume his post with the *Oracle*. Chilton, Ryall, and Paterson had naturally assumed that Southwell would rejoin them when he left Bristol jail in January 1843. Instead of doing so, Southwell preferred to launch a new journal, the *Investigator*, a publication which would demonstrate the falsehoods of Christianity without shocking the Christian masses. Having purposely sustained the *Oracle* for Southwell's reappearance, Chilton and Ryall were understandably annoyed but nevertheless vowed to see the *Oracle*, whose circulation had diminished considerably, through to the completion of the volume.

In Holyoake's opinion, the *Oracle* had declined in quality. He despised sensationalism. When the *Oracle* spoke crudely of the Royal family, and when it advocated the "systematic assassination" of parsons in Ireland as the quickest means of freeing Ireland from Protestant rule, Holyoake let his feelings be known.[50]   If the priests were to be destroyed, reason should be the only weapon. Not only was such journalism irresponsible, but it also displayed a lack of faith in the principle of reason itself. In July Holyoake admitted that "it has been suggested to me that I should have no more to do with the *Oracle*."[51]   To break with friends over such differences of opinion, however, was not Holyoake's way. Moreover, he had become very involved in the Anti-Persecution Union which depended upon the *Oracle* for publicity.

Ryall had systematized the procedure for collection of funds to defend these freethinkers and their families who had fallen victim to persecution. The *Oracle* alone advertised the Union's meetings and reported the amounts collected. During the summer of 1843, Holyoake assumed the post of secretary of the Union. With Southwell and Holyoake both out of jail, there seemed to be little reason for the Union's continued existence, but Holyoake proposed that the Union should be sustained in order that it could render speedy assistance in case of more legal trouble.[52]

Events soon proved Holyoake correct. When two Edinburgh booksellers were arrested in July for selling the works of Paine and Voltaire, the Union rallied immediately to their support. Also, in the summer of 1843, Robert Kalley, a Scottish Protestant physician, who had been living in Portugal for some years, was arrested by the

Madeira police for speaking against the doctrines of Roman Catholicism.[53]   When Holyoake learned of the incident, he initiated correspondence with Kalley and assured him that the Union defended atheist and Christian alike from persecution.[54]   Ironically, Thomas Paterson was himself arrested when he appeared at an Edinburgh meeting for Kalley's defense which was sponsored by orthodox Christians.

The Anti-Persecution Union now had plenty to do but was hardly in any position to lend anyone much more than moral support. Because the Union was so closely associated with the anti-Owenite *Oracle*, the majority of the Socialists would have nothing to do with it. For their reluctance to respond to the Union's appeals, the Socialists incurred Holyoake's wrath. They, he wrote, cared nothing for basic human rights and liberties, while the Anti-Persecution Union regarded as "gross injustice," any interference with the expression of opinion.[55] The truth of the matter was that the Socialists had no money to give, especially to such a small operation.

By the fall of 1843, the days of the *Oracle* were numbered. After Paterson's arrest, Chilton edited the second volume of the *Oracle* under his own name. In the preface which he affixed to the *Oracle's* second volume, Chilton revealed that, after an initial figure of 4,000, circulation had quickly been reduced to approximately 700. The second volume would never have seen completion had not W.J. Birch, a freethinking Shakespearean scholar from Oxford, guaranteed a generous subsidy. Birch, probably introduced into free thought and Socialist circles by Southwell, later became an important benefactor of Holyoake. Thus, the *Oracle of Reason*, begun as an act of civil disobedience and to counter the *New Moral World*, expired with a final claim that it had given atheism a "local habitation and a name among the working classes."[56]

The *Oracle's* poor circulation was partly a result of the depression when workingmen had not a spare penny. Because the journal had been devoted to Socialist squabbling and theological criticism, it would have been difficult to reach a wider public even under more favorable economic circumstances. Two weeks before the *Oracle's* demise, Holyoake gave notice of a new journal, the *Movement*. As its prospectus explained, the *Movement* would be a continuation of the *Oracle*. Supernaturalism, or religion, would be denounced and philosophic materialism would be defended as the only foundation of thought and action.[57]   With the cooperation of

Ryall, Holyoake published the first number of the *Movement* on December 16, 1843.

Subscribers were soon informed that Socialism was also to be one of the *Movement's* concerns. More convinced than ever that the Socialists erred by ignoring atheism or free thought, Holyoake explained that the *Movement* would

> add theology to political economy. The errors of the priests are not less dangerous than the mistakes of the capitalists. Socialism will be criticized in the *Movement*, but not in the spirit of antagonism. The present policy of the Socialists I think not correct— the measures neither so vigorous nor practical as they might be; but they *may* be correct. I arrogate no infallibility; I only venture to explain differences. I question not the Central Board's integrity—assume no dishonesty; I only impugn their judgment, and desire if indeed I am able, to improve, not condemn.[58]

Hoping to gain more Socialist readers than had the *Oracle*, Holyoake emphasized that his criticism of Socialism was to be entirely constructive. The unsound policies to which he referred were, of course, the retreat in the face of clerical assault and the attempt to create a paradise in the Hampshire countryside. Furthermore, Holyoake believed that it was a serious mistake for Owenism to become so narrowly defined. Not until men were freed from the doctrines of sin, guilt and absolute dependence on God could they hope to create equitable social institutions. Therefore, before capitalism was destroyed, Christianity must be brought low.

The Socialists, Holyoake continued, had profited from the atheists despite their unpleasant association. Judged once as a most disreputable lot, the Socialists had risen in public esteem by comparison with their anti-theological brethren. Their respectability, however, had done them great harm. Of all reformers dedicated to society's readjustment, the Socialists, Holyoake explained, had the most comprehensive and radical objectives. Socialist assumptions regarding behavior, knowledge and the nature of man were such that few nineteenth century Christians could have found them acceptable. The philosophy of Locke and Hume, joined to a Rousseauist faith in the basic goodness of natural man, had become popularized in Socialism. But the Owenites approached their task with extraordinary apathy. Instead of capitalizing on their truth, Owen, Lloyd Jones and the *New Moral World* were smothering Socialist doctrines in the "wretched nomenclature of orthodoxy." No worse result could be achieved, Holyoake believed, than for Socialist and Christian minds to meet. He concluded his rather comprehensive critique with a statement which would have been acceptable to most non-Socialist Christians. "No religious man can be a Socialist." [59]

The *New Moral World* replied to such criticism by asking what positive contribution to progress these self-labeled atheists were prepared to make. To take the opportunity to weigh the principles of atheism in the "balance of utility," returned Holyoake, was exactly what he desired to do.[60]   Atheism, he asserted, destroyed all utopias, all millenarianism. "The less we think of other worlds, the more we think of this—the less we hope of the future, the greater is our anxiety to rationalize, to improve, and increase the happiness of the present."[61]   Religion kept man ignorant, superstitious and bigoted. Its "infamous and degrading coils" must be removed by knowledge and reason before the goodness of men could appear. The Socialists might have accomplished this had their effectiveness not been crippled because they had accepted the one feature of the Enlightment—faith in progress—which undermined their other assumptions about man's nature and development. The Socialists had become so concerned with the new moral world, especially as it became objectified in the Hampshire countryside, that they had fallen into the same category as complacent Christians who, looking forward to eternal bliss, were ignorant and apathetic about the conditions in which they actually existed. Atheism could demonstrate that it was on themselves alone, not their dreams, that men must rely. Stripped of faith in mysterious revelation and utopias, human beings could discover their true potential and restrict their objectives to that which was realistically attainable.

As the Congress of 1844 drew near, Holyoake called on the Socialists to consider a number of issues. First, what besides the Queenwood colony were the Socialists doing about home colonization? Such enormous costs meant that Socialists would have to seek financial aid. Was it not ridiculous for Owen to assume that the wealthy would lend the Socialists money for "breaking up the [capitalist] foundation of society?" If the Socialists seriously intended to build communities, Congress must discover how the working class could do so independently. Secondly, would the

Socialist leadership continue to treat the working classes as children? "Paternalism," Holyoake declared, "is a great evil because it deludes men with talk of freedom."[62] Up to this moment, he continued, the laboring classes have been falsely impressed with the wealth of the middle classes and by Owen's call to a unity which cut across class lines. Finally, Holyoake asked if Congress would devote any discussion to atheism. Because some Socialists believed their organization to be atheistic, a discussion of policy toward Christianity should be on the agenda. Holyoake never expected, however, that his queries would appear on their agenda, not when urgent questions of finance and the direction of the farm existed.

When Congress met at the end of May, Holyoake's attention was diverted from its proceedings by the first of several conflicts he would have with Charles Southwell. Southwell was such a vain man that when Holyoake had given special praise to Thomas Paterson for being a foe of Christianity, Southwell was so displeased that he wrote a series of complaining letters to Holyoake.[63] This exchange revealed the lack of harmony among the little group of atheist Socialists. It was, however, insignificant compared to the storm which erupted among the Socialists gathered at Queenwood. Many delegates had come to question the financial and agricultural management of the farm and neither the Central Board nor Owen were able to placate them.

Since its purchase in 1839, the colony had experienced vacillating fortunes. First, Owen had refused to act as governor of the community because Queenwood was occupied by only a preliminary working party.[64] John Finch of Liverpool, on Owen's recommendation, was appointed acting governor. During the first two years the original enthusiasm cooled very quickly. Even though applicants were carefully screened, they possessed too few agricultural skills to operate the farm successfully. By the summer of 1840, their numbers had dwindled from 57 to only 19. Financial difficulties haunted the experiment from the very beginning because the Socialist societies could never hope to raise the thousands of pounds necessary for Queenwood's development. Had not a few wealthy Socialists, organized in 1840 by Owen into the "Home Colonization Society," lent substantial sums to the Central Board, the construction of Harmony Hall could not have begun.

In 1841 Owen began to direct affairs and was granted unlimited control of funds. Instead of making needed improvements, Owen had Harmony Hall erected at the cost of £30,000. Designed to house the residents of Queenwood, Harmony Hall was a truly magnificent structure built of the finest quality materials complete with mahogany paneling and a conveyor system which operated between dining room and kitchen. By 1843 the *New Moral World* was able to present more heartening financial reports but they were of very questionable veracity. Moreover, life within Queenwood was increasingly spartan. Now, Owen appealed to the local societies for an additional £25,000 to complete construction of his domain's facilities.

Local Socialist societies, many of which were in debt for their own Halls of Science, were understandably irritated by the appeals of the Central Board. Those men and women who had lived for a time in the colony did not always return with the most favorable reports of the conditions which they experienced. Moreover, the missionaries, whose salaries had been sacrificed to Queenwood in 1842, were no longer available to stimulate local enthusiasm or function as a liason between the societies and the Central Board. Now, many of the delegates who assembled at Harmony Hall represented societies which believed that they were being neglected and exploited.

At these meetings, Owen was customarily elected to the post of chairman. This time precedent was overturned. John Finch, returned from a trip to the United States, reluctantly presided as the delegates carefully scrutinized Owen's managerial record. As a result of this investigation, a number of regulations for the operation of Queenwood were enacted. Outraged at this effrontery, Owen came forward and announced that "he could not accept office in connection with the Society, unless he could have free authority to act as circumstances rendered it necessary, without reference to previous resolutions of Congress." [65] As much as they venerated Owen, these delegates were not prepared to submit to his continued despotism. Owen resigned, and after much debate, John Buxton, a delegate from Manchester, was elected President and governor of Harmony. Unfortunately, the election of Buxton who, as well as anyone there, represented the dissatisfaction of the local societies, divided the Socialists. The old members of the Central Board— those who had supported Owen completely and had themselves invested £3,000 in Queenwood—refused to serve with Buxton. In effect, there were now two executive boards.

Many Socialists interpreted these resignations as an attempt to destroy the power of Buxton and the new board. Some, such as Isaac

Ironside of Sheffield, turned to Holyoake's *Movement* because "of its circulation being generally amongst Socialists" to publicize their charges that the old Central Board had practiced "deceit, duplicity, and dishonesty."[66]   Actually, Holyoake was not immediately impressed by the events which had taken place in the late Congress. He congratulated the delegates for not passing the usual fare of cut-and-dried resolutions but criticized the meeting for having ignored the issue of atheism.[67]   William Galpin responded with a patronizing letter, advising Holyoake "never [to] oppose unless you see an extreme necessity for it."[68]   During June and July 1844, Holyoake's attention was consumed by the Anti-Persecution Union. Paterson was still in jail and Holyoake could think of little else than encouraging the *Movement's* readers to support the Union and to petition Parliament to repeal the blasphemy laws.

It was not until Owen left Britain for the United States in August 1844 that the *Movement* turned full attention to Socialism. It would be foolish, Holyoake advised Buxton, to speak of "universal interests" and "charity for all" as did the old Central Board. Rather than submit to middle class direction, the laboring class must direct its own progress.[69]   "Community" takes on a new meaning in the pages of the *Movement.* No longer does Holyoake use the term in reference to an actual institution; rather, "community" designates working class unity, cooperation and consciousness. There is no mention of the millennium; Holyoake cared little at this point about changing the world. He never attempted to destroy the grandiose vision of Owen, but he believed that the colony at Queenwood and Owen's emphasis on class cooperation were obscuring the true interest of the lower orders. Before true Socialism could be realized, they had to become spiritually and politically emancipated.

On October 14, 1844, Holyoake set out from London to inspect the Queenwood farm in order that he might be able to found his opinions on first-hand observations. "The soil," he observed upon arriving, "has *now* been made productive at a great expense. The more a stranger gazes on that estate, the more he wonders at the sagacity which first selected it, and he comes to the conclusion that it was chosen with an eye to insolvency..." His reports were obviously intended to discredit the old Central Board. The use of expensive furnishings at Harmony Hall was denounced as a "monument of ill-timed magnificence" and a testimony to Owen's pretentiousness. Holyoake noted also that the living conditions which he observed did seem more agreeable under the present management than had been previously reported. Buxton governed far more democratically than Owen or John Finch; now at least there were no separate tables in the dining hall for the managers.[70]

Holyoake concluded his report by expressing genuine optimism regarding the future of the colony now that Owen's influence had been reduced. Instead of creating a new world the communists there were devoted to making the experiment succeed. Had Holyoake been content to describe the Queenwood situation as he found it, little or no hostility toward himself would have been created. In his concluding article, he again accused the "back-bone Owenites" of deliberately trying to sabotage the efforts of the newly elected executive by withdrawing their support. Owen, Lloyd Jones and all connected with the *New Moral World* were accused of faithlessness. [71] Such pen lashings did not greatly disturb the Socialists but Holyoake tried to strengthen his criticism by insinuating that the governor prior to Buxton (he is probably referring to John Finch and not to Robert Owen) was guilty of embezzling funds. Apparently, £ 500 had been lent to the colony by Finch. Out of power, he demanded his money back and got it. Holyoake claimed that he had examined the financial records at Harmony and could find no reference to the initial transaction. Finch, he hinted, might well be trying to fleece his fellow communists.

Although the Owenites stressed the role of environment in character formation, they tended to be quite egotistical. They could accept the most devastating critique of their philosophy or utopian projects without being upset. When their character was impugned, however, or if they were accused of personal dishonesty, they would rise immediately to retort. Lloyd Jones, in his defense of John Finch, accused Holyoake of purposeful misrepresentation and urged that association with Holyoake be ended by the Socialists.[72] Even many of those who were dissatisfied with Owen's guidance agreed that Holyoake's accusations bordered on being libelous. Recognizing that he did not have sufficient evidence to make a convincing case for embezzlement, Holyoake immediately wrote a slightly revised edition of his Harmony reports in which he admitted that all transactions had been properly, if not altogether adequately, recorded. [73]

The admission, however, was not enough to keep Holyoake out of serious trouble. Branch A1 in London, the most prosperous and influential of all the Socialist societies, placed the question of G.J. Holyoake and his accusations at the top of their agenda during

December 1844 and January 1845. The Harmony reports, they
stated, had "an evil tendency, inasmuch as they malign the character of others and are not altogether founded upon the truth."[74]
Holyoake was accused of misrepresentation and of trying to make
the existing differences between Socialists completely unbridgeable.
Unpacified by Holyoake's amended report which they felt "contained but a reiteration of the falsehoods before exposed," the
members of Branch A1 passed a vote of censure on Holyoake's
conduct.[75] This action was very significant. If allowed to stand,
their decision would have branded Holyoake a liar—a man whose
opinions could not be trusted by those who had the highest regard
for unrestricted freedom of expression. For all practical purposes,
Holyoake had been expelled from the Rational Society.

A large minority of the membership of Branch A1 did consider
the act of censure unnecessary. Having made his retraction,
Holyoake continued to maintain that his articles regarding Harmony
had been substantially true and without malice. On January 12,
Henry Hetherington, a London Chartist and the publisher who had
led the struggle for an unstamped press, rose to rescind the motion
of censure. After a debate which filled the Sunday morning
program, the meeting adjourned. Hetherington immediately contacted Holyoake and requested any additional information which
might aid in clearing his name.[76] Why Hetherington took such an
interest in defending Holyoake is not certain. Holyoake's friendli-
ness to the Chartists was no secret; in addition, Hetherington, who
was also a Socialist, had published Holyoake's amended Harmony
report, and he shared many of Holyoake's opinions of Owen. On
January 19, 1845, Branch A1 considered the issue once again.
Finally, it was agreed to delete the point of censure and simply
express "regret that Mr. Holyoake did not make the proper
enquiries before he published his statement."[77] A further amendment was offered to reinsert a statement of censure but when it
failed by a slim majority of three, the matter was finally dropped. In
spite of this controversy, Holyoake's reputation had not been too
severely damaged. He had also learned another important lesson
about professional journalism: to print accusations is very unwise.

During February, Holyoake had become ill. The nature of this
illness is uncertain, but Holyoake's vision, always weak, was very
seriously affected. This was not to be the first time that his career
would be threatened by near blindness. For most of February and
March 1845, Holyoake was confined to bed, unable to carry on with

his lectures or attend to the *Movement*. On April 2, the *Movement* announced that it would cease publication. When the second volume had commenced in January, the *Movement* had contracted a debt of but 7. Now, the sum of his indebtedness had risen to £ 25. Holyoake had a phobia about being in debt and he refused, therefore, to allow the *Movement* to continue. It was not, he insisted, the apathy of Socialists or atheists which brought about the end of the *Movement*. Although its circulation could never have exceeded 1,000, Holyoake blamed his own absence, resulting from illness, for the unfortunate financial condition. The *Movement* and the *Oracle of Reason*, Holyoake was proud to say, had given bigotry worthy opponents. Free thought itself had assumed a new character. "In periodicals and lectures, in courts of law in conventional England and sanctimonious Scotland, the voice of undisguised Atheism has been heard." Holyoake also had some parting words for Socialists:

> Once the waters of Socialism ran through the land
> in refreshing fertilizing streams but at last settled
> into a respectable and stagnant pool, giving forth
> only the unhealthy effluvia of conventionality,
> jesuitry, and religion. To stir and sweeten this
> water, to open the sluices again which carries its
> streams by the poor man's cottage had been with us
> an earnest work.[78]

With these sentiments, the *Movement* concluded. In May 1845 Holyoake left for Glasgow where he had accepted a temporary post as lecturer to the Glasgow Rational Society. The two ephemeral journals with which Holyoake had been associated did not really give much new life to either atheism or socialism. Like many other short-lived journals of the 1830s and 1840s which called the working classes to action, the *Oracle* and *Movement* could not continue because so few could afford to subscribe to them. The prosperity of the 1850s would bring forth new readers and new journals as well.

While Holyoake was in Glasgow with his family, life must have been very grim. The Glasgow Socialists were as poor in spirit as in things substantial. The Holyoakes were already conditioned to meagre subsistence but in Glasgow Holyoake could do nothing to excite a response from the Socialists. During these months, Holyoake wrote *Rationalism, a Treatise for the Times*, a lengthy tract in which he deplored the fatalism which had infected Socialism. In the late summer, Holyoake also received the news of

Ryall's death. The two men had been very close friends for the past two years and his passing was a great blow to Holyoake. When Holyoake's next son was born, he named him Malthus Questall in honor of his devoted assistant. Added to this sadness were reports that Thomas Paterson and Southwell had become bitter enemies. Holyoake, however, was not the only person with difficulties. The Socialist Congress of 1845, disheartened by financial reports, had decided to close Queenwood.

During the summer of 1845, the few remaining communists were sent home. John Buxton and his family stayed on at Harmony as caretakers. Writing from Harmony Hall in the summer of 1845, John Crane, the last secretary of the Socialist Congress, expressed these feelings:

> I can scarcely persuade myself that time is a reality. I look back on what we have been and what we are; we were a Society intent for the holiest of purposes; we had a leader in whom we reposed the most unbounded confidence—nay by many of us he was almost worshipped, and all were ready to follow to the death for the accomplishment of our object... and now we are disjointed, cast down and powerless. [79]

Certainly he was articulating the mood of those Owenites who had committed their energy and fortunes to the Queenwood project. It is true also that many of Owen's disciples had placed altogether too much faith in their old prophet. The passion to build communities had finally expired. On the other hand, many Owenites had never been directly involved with the project. With this albatross removed, the way was cleared for new men and for new interpretations of Owenism. Queenwood still had to be sold and, ironically, the controversy created over the disposition of the property would draw Holyoake back into a position of some importance within the Socialist movement.

There was no future for Holyoake in Glasgow. His friend and publisher, James Watson, tried to help by finding Holyoake a position as a teacher in London. Watson also believed that the demise of the *New Moral World* in January 1846 had created a vacuum which a new publication might profitably fill. [80] Such a journal, wrote Watson, would have to be broad enough in its appeal to attract a wide readership. There would be literary pieces, scientific articles and, of course, discussion of all social questions. By including such articles, it was not inconceivable that a few middle class patrons could be attracted.

The new journal should also inform the laboring classes that morality was independent of religion. Atheists or freethinkers, and later the Secularists, were far from being libertines. While they were opposed to all religious dogma on the grounds that it despoiled the human spirit, they were very concerned that the laboring poor acquire a rather strict code of morality. Drunkenness, ignorance and idleness were condemned, not as sins against God but as offenses against society. Although society was held originally responsible for men's vice, individuals must be encouraged to transcend their environmental conditioning. The faith of reformers like Watson and Holyoake was that men could, if encouraged and instructed, free themselves of the poverty—ignorance—poverty cycle. Morality would eventually find its natural base in the individual's recognition of his duty toward humanity.

Finally, Watson envisioned that a well-edited periodical could perhaps reunite the Socialists, many of whom were considering emigration as a solution to their failure in Britain.[81]   If Holyoake decided to accept this offer, Watson promised that he would have full control as editor, and all proceeds which might accrue would be Holyoake's. Although Watson conducted an active publishing business, he could not, however, afford the initial cost of beginning a new journal.

The capital came from an unexpected source. While in Glasgow, Holyoake had joined the Oddfellows Society. In the fall of 1845, the Manchester Lodge sponsored an essay contest asking each entrant to write a short lecture on his choice of five topics: Charity, Truth, Knowledge, Science and Progress. Having little to do in Glasgow, Holyoake decided to compete and submitted an essay on each topic, hoping that a unified presentation would stand well with the judges. He left Scotland for London in the spring of 1846 and one day was surprised when the Grand Master of Oddfellows paid him a visit and awarded him £ 50 for having presented the best essay in each category. With this sum, the *Reasoner* was begun.[82] Once again, Holyoake had a journal. He also took upon himself the tasks which Watson had suggested, especially the reunification of the divided and discouraged Socialists.

NOTES TO CHAPTER TWO

1 *New Moral World*, VII, No. 20 (November 14, 1840), 316.

2 Holyoake, *Log Book No. 1* (December, 1840), B.I.

3 *Ibid.* (June 30, 1840), B.I.

4 *Ibid.* (March, 1841), B.I.

5 *New Moral World*, IX, No. 3 (January 16, 1840), and *New Moral World*, IX, No. 20 (May 15, 1841), 310.

6 Joseph Barker, *The Abominations of Socialism Exposed* (Newcastle: J. Blackwell and Co., 1840), p. 2.

7 Holyoake submitted lengthy accounts of his activities in the defense of Socialism to the *New Moral World*. See Vol. IX (1841).

8 *New Moral World*, IX, No. 24 (June 12, 1841), 367.

9 Holyoake to Eleanor Holyoake (May 18, 1841), No. 19, C.U.

10 Holyoake, *Log Book No. 1* (June, 1841), and (July, 1841), B.I.

11 Walter Newall to Holyoake, *Letterbook* (July 15,1841), B.I.

12 Great Britain, *Hansard's Parliamentary Debates*, LI (1840), 510-532. See also G.C.B. Davies, *Henry Phillpotts, Bishop of Exeter* (London: SPCK, 1954) pp. 338-40.

13 *Hansard*, LI (1840), 1186.

14 *New Moral World*, VI, No. 38 (July 11, 1839), 593.

15 *Ibid.*, IX, No. 23 (June 6, 1841), 351.

16 *Oracle of Reason*, No. 1 (November 6, 1841), pp. 1-2.

17 Holyoake, *Sixty Years*, I, 142. See Chilton's statement about Holyoake in *Oracle of Reason*, preface to Vol. II (December, 1843), iii-v.

18 *Oracle of Reason*, No. 4 (November 27, 1841), p. 25.

19 William Carpenter, *The Trial of Charles Southwell for Blasphemy* (London: Hetherington, 1842). Carpenter had been specifically engaged by Malthus Ryall to report the trial. He was paid by collections taken among sympathetic Socialists.

20 *Oracle of Reason*, No. 5 (December 4, 1841), p. 33.

21 Charles Southwell, *Socialism Made Easy* (London: James Watson, 1840), p. 13.

22 *Oracle of Reason*, No. 5 (December 4, 1841), p. 33.

23 *New Moral World*, X, No. 24 (December 11, 1841), 191.

24 G.J. Holyoake, *The Advantages and Disadvantages of Trades Unions* (Sheffield: Hardcastle, 1842), p. 12.

25 William Chilton to Holyoake (December 16, 1841), No. 22, C.U.

26 Malthus Ryall to Holyoake (January 4, 1842), No. 24, C.U.

27 *Oracle of Reason*, No. 8 (February 12, 1842), pp. 65-66.

28 Charles Southwell to Holyoake (February 19, 1842), No. 25, C.U.

29 *Oracle of Reason*, No. 10 (February 26, 1842), pp. 81-82.

30 *Ibid.*, No. 16 (April 9, 1942), p. 129.

31 *Ibid.*, No. 23 (May 12, 1842), p. 186.

32 H. Jeffrey to Holyoake (March 23, 1842), No. 32, and (April 7, 1842), No. 37, C.U.

33 William Galpin to Holyoake (March 14, 1842), No. 29, C.U.

34 William Galpin to Holyoake (March 22, 1842), No. 31, C.U.

35 McCabe, *Life and Letters of Holyoake*, I, 63. McCabe believed that

the question was put deliberately in order to trap Holyoake into blasphemy. Although the trial record did show that there were hostile persons present, there is no evidence that the question was asked deceitfully.

36 *Oracle of Reason*, No. 24 (June 4, 1842), p. 200. Holyoake's reply is recorded differently in various accounts although the substance is the same. I chose the *Oracle*'s version because it was the account written closest to the event and it was probably written by Holyoake himself.

37 William Galpin to A. Parker (June 6, 1842), No. 47, C.U.

38 *Oracle of Reason*, No. 27 (June 25, 1842), pp. 221-26.

39 *Ibid.*, No. 28 (July 2, 1942), pp. 225-26.

40 *Ibid.*, No. 30 (July 16, 1842), p. 241.

41 *Ibid.*, No. 34 (August 13, 1842), pp. 273-74.

42 Great Britain, *Hansard's Parliamentary Debates*, LXV (1842), 243.

43 William Galpin to Holyoake (July 4, 1842), No. 54, C.U.

44 Richard Carlile to Holyoake (August 16, 1842), No. 66, C.U.

45 For a complete account of the proceedings including Holyoake's elaborate defense see Anti-Persecution Union, *The Trial of George Jacob Holyoake on an Indictment of Blasphemy* (London: T. Paterson, 1842). As in the case of Southwell, a secretary was hired to make a transcript of the trial.

46 G.J. Holyoake, *History of the Last Trial by Jury for Atheism in England* (London: J. Watson, 1850) contains a very embellished account of his imprisonment. See Holyoake, *Sixty Years*, I, 164-75 for a condensed version.

47 G.J. Holyoake, *A Short and Easy Method with the Saints* (London: Hetherington, 1843), p. 28.

48 See G.J. Holyoake, *Paley Refuted in His Own Words* (London: Hetherington and Co., 1843).

49 *Oracle of Reason*, No. 65 (March 11, 1843), p. 97.

50 *Ibid.*, No. 78 (June 10, 1843), p. 202.

51 *Ibid.*, No. 81 (July 1, 1843), p. 231.

52 *Ibid.*, No. 82 (July 8, 1843), pp. 233-35.

53 *Narrative of Circumstances connected with the Confinement of Dr. Robert Reid Kalley*, by an English Resident (London: J. Hatchard and Son, 1844). Anonymous pamphlet presents interesting details of the diplomatic aspects of this incident.

54 Their correspondence began in August 1843 and continued for several months. Although longwinded, it illustrates the strength of Holyoake's conviction that knowledge of a supernatural being was impossible.

55 *Oracle of Reason*, No. 98 (October 28, 1843), pp. 359-60.

56 *Ibid.*, preface to Vol. II (December, 1843), pp. iii-v.

57 *Ibid.*, No. 101 (November 18, 1843), p. 389.

58 *Movement*, No. 3 (December 30, 1843), p. 389.

59 *Ibid.*, No. 7 (January 27, 1844), p. 51.

60 *Ibid.*, No. 12 (March 2, 1844), pp. 89-90.

61 *Ibid.*, No. 7 (January 27, 1844), p. 51.

62 *Ibid.*, No. 18 (April 13, 1844), pp. 137-40.

63 Southwell to Holyoake (May 18, 1844; May 23, 1844; May 24, 1844), Nos. 117, 118, 119, C.U.

64 Much of the following account may be found in Podmore, *Robert Owen*, II, 530-74. His narrative is based almost exclusively upon information contained in the *New Moral World*.

65 Podmore, *Robert Owen*, II, 557.

66 Isaac Ironside to Holyoake (June 3, 1844), No. 121, C.U.

67 *Movement*, No. 27 (June 15, 1844), pp. 209-10.

68 William Galpin to Holyoake (June 16, 1844), No. 122, C.U.

69 *Movement*, No. 36 (August 17, 1844), p. 287.

70 *Ibid.*, No. 47 (October 30, 1844), p. 403 and No. 48 (November 6, 1844), pp. 409-13.

71 *Ibid.*, No. 49 (November 13, 1844), pp. 417-19.

72 *Ibid.*, No. 51 (November 27, 1844), p. 438.

73 Holyoake, *A Visit to Harmony Hall* (London: H. Hetherington, 1844), p. 13.

74 *New Moral World*, XIII, No. 25 (December 13, 1844), 198.

75 *Ibid.*, No. 28 (January 4, 1845), 222.

76 Henry Hetherington to Holyoake (January 14, 1845), No. 138, C.U.

77 *New Moral World*, XIII, No. 13 (January 25, 1845), 246.

78 *Movement*, No. 68 (April 2, 1845), pp. 105-106.

79 Podmore, *Robert Owen*, II, 572.

80 James Watson to Holyoake (February 27, 1846), No. 159, C.U.

81 James Watson to Holyoake (March 12, 1846), No. 161, C.U.

82 Holyoake, *Sixty Years*, I, 204-08.

CHAPTER III

SCATTERED FRIENDS OF PROGRESS

Mid-century British radicalism was composed of several strains; besides the disillusioned Owenites, there were the Chartists and the middle class radicals represented in Parliament by men such as John Bright and Joseph Hume. To these groups must be added the small but notorious cliques of freethinkers and atheists. All agreed that British politics must be rationalized, that aristocratic influence be reduced and that society be harmonized by bestowing political rights and dignity upon the laboring class. But, at this point, agreement ended.

The various radical factions found coalition well near impossible because each was suspicious of the goals and motives of the others. For example, Chartists suspected that Parliamentary radicals were concerned with the Charter only to the extent that it might somehow benefit the interests of industrial Manchester. Each group also had to contend with further fragmentation because, like the Chartists, each had its moderate wing and each its more militant faction which sought immediate realization of goals even at the risk of fostering reaction. Although the fact of working class consciousness has been well established, there was a definite absence of party unity on a number of vital issues.

One characteristic of Victorian intellectuals, as Walter Houghton has illustrated, was the rigidity with which they held to their beliefs.[1] Political and social radicals were no different. Conviction can indeed bind men toegether but, as Holyoake soon discovered, working-class radicalism was denominationalized by dogmatic disagreement. Radicalism may be understood only by reference to its numerous factions, clustered around personalities and regions as often as convictions. In 1846 the freethinking Holyoake set out to resuscitate British Socialism. Before the emergence of Secularism in 1852, he would have occasion to become more broadly involved with other segments of radicalism. As he became somewhat more prominent, chiefly because of the *Reasoner*, Holyoake's own attitudes toward reform experienced a rather remarkable but not altogether atypical transformation. He was to learn that the impediments to working class progress were great indeed and that these obstacles lay without the various orders of radicalism as well as in the structure of British society and government.

By 1846, Holyoake's competency as a working class journalist had considerably improved. The experience with the *Oracle* and the *Movement* enabled him to write quickly and in a style which appealed to working class readers.[2]   He continued to avoid the extremes of pompous intellectualism and vulgar sensationalism. The *Reasoner*, in which he uninterruptedly presented his opinions for fifteen years, also serves a biographer well for it is his private diary made public.[3]

The *Reasoner* was first issued on June 3, 1846. In his opening editorial, Holyoake announced that the *Reasoner* would be "Communistic in Social Economy—Utilitarian in Morals—Republican in Politics—and Anti-Theological in Religion."[4]   Continuing the tradition of the *Oracle* and the *Movement*, the main objective of the *Reasoner* would be to confront theology with reason. Quite correctly Holyoake began by placing British free thought in the activist-materialist tradition emanating from Diderot and Paine. More akin to the *philosophes* than to their German contemporaries such as Ludwig Feuerbach and D.F. Strauss, British freethinkers rejected German philosophic materialism and higher Biblical criticism because it seemed so abstruse. Theological criticism, however, was quickly deferred to Socialist affairs in the *Reasoner* because Watson encouraged Holyoake to give maximum editorial attention to Socialism.

Watson also insisted that the *Herald of Progress*, the gazette of the Rational Society since the demise of the *New Moral World*, be bound with the *Reasoner*. Although Holyoake encouraged the Socialists to shake off their despondency, there was scant hope for reviving Owenism. When the Central Board, for example, on which Holyoake now functioned as general secretary, announced that members who paid but one shilling would be reinstated with all dues in arrears forgiven, merely 187 persons, scattered among twenty towns, responded. Only London, Sheffield, and Leicester could boast societies of twenty members.[5]

The one matter yet to be settled was the disposition of the

Hampshire property. In 1845 the Socialist congress had rid itself of Queenwood by transferring control of the property to designated assignees. John Buxton, the ex-governor, was to remain on the premises until a settlement was made. Although an honorable man, Buxton had little experience with financial and legal procedures. He was also convinced that cooperation with members of the former Central Board, who maintained thay they were the legal trustees of Queenwood, was impossible because of the attitude which they had taken at the time of his election. In early June 1846, John Finch, acting within his right as a trustee, had Buxton and his family evicted on the grounds that their continued presence was preventing disposition of the property. Believing an injustice done, Buxton erected a tent outside the premises and remained there in protest.[6] The new Central Board, Holyoake included, condemned Finch for his action.

A special congress attended by less than twenty persons met on June 29 to settle the matter. At this confused and acrimonious gathering, it was finally agreed that the trustees and John Finch had acted legally. Buxton was called upon to cooperate and, soon after, Harmony Hall was rented to a Mr. George Edmunson who founded there Queenwood College.[7] In Holyoake's opinion, the relinquishing of Harmony Hall was a step forward. With the cause of so much frustration and bitterness removed, the remaining Socialists might unite. After July 1846 no rancorous communications were printed in the *Reasoner*. By appearing on the rostrum at the dedication of the Finsbury Mechanics' Institution with G.A. Fleming, the former editor of the *New Moral World*, Holyoake demonstrated that he was willing to bury past quarrels.[8] This ceremony itself was symbolic because the building had formerly belonged to the Finsbury Rational Society. Elsewhere, similar developments transpired. In London the fine structure which the Rational Society had built was converted from a Hall of Science to the John Street Literary and Scientific Institution. For the time being, organized Socialism in Great Britain was non-existent, but now the possibilities seemed greater for new and less visionary projects.

The immediate result of these affairs was the near ruin of the *Reasoner*. Watson had hoped that the journal would do well as the single Socialist publication. But, so few were the Socialists that the *Reasoner's* circulation did not exceed 1,500 and was probably closer to 1,000. Furthermore, the *Reasoner* had yielded too much space in its early weeks of publication to disgruntled Socialists to attract a wider public. In September, an effort was made to minimize losses by reducing the size of the *Reasoner* from sixteen pages to eight and its price from two to one and one-half pence. Nevertheless, costs continued to exceed income and it appeared that the *Reasoner* would soon have to be discontinued.[9]   If the *Reasoner* were to succeed in drawing together the disenchanted Socialists, it first had to survive.

The task which Holyoake had accepted was too great for a journal alone to accomplish. During the next several years, Holyoake tried to create a society to seek those objectives which the *Reasoner* advocated. In October 1846 he proclaimed the creation of the Society for the Promulgation of Naturalism. The single purpose of this society was to oppose the "vast, organized error" of religion.[10] Essentially, the Rational Society would have been recreated unencumbered by Communism. When Holyoake received no response or encouragement, he decided that "naturalism" was an unfortunate name to have chosen and quietly abandoned the project.

In December he announced the formation of the Society of Theological Utilitarians. Soon known as the Utilitarian Society, this association was dedicated to the "extirpation of the grosser religions and the refutation of the refined ones." Holyoake must have realized that few men would be attracted by such dull business, but he was still persuaded that social inequities were founded upon religion. By freeing society from domination by priests and their dehumanizing doctrines, the Utilitarian Society would "not negate political agitation, nor supersede social reform but [would become] the handmaid and helpmate of both. [11]

The Utilitarian Society held its first meeting—an ill-attended affair at the John Street Institution—on April 11, 1847. Each week, the *Utilitarian Record*, which was appended to the *Reasoner*, reported the weekly meetings of the society, advertised lectures being given at other working class literary clubs about London, and announced the penny publications of the London radical press. Although the Utilitarian Society lingered on until mid-1848, it never became involved in any activities outside the lecture room or made an effort to gain many members. The society did, however, foster contact among a very small group of Owenites, freethinkers and a few Chartists who congregated regularly at the John Street Institution. Ineffective as it may have been, the Utilitarian Society did keep Holyoake from despairing that some progress toward a more effective organization could be made.

The financial position of the *Reasoner* at the conclusion of its first year of publication was distressing. Unless extreme measures were taken immediately to increase income, Watson would have no choice but to halt publication. In June 1847 Holyoake made a forthright appeal to his readers for financial support. Hoping to secure approximately £ 50, he explained that the *Reasoner* could continue if each subscriber would contribute one shilling. Holyoake was not begging, and he was not discouraged by the apparent apathy which necessitated this appeal. Laboring men, he believed, must be enlightened even if they did not naturally desire or support such efforts. If his few readers were truly men of principle, and if they really desired progress, they would sustain the one journal in Britain which sought to destroy the crippling bonds of Christianity.[12]

The response was surprising. By June 9, 1847, 391 shillings had been collected; a week later, the total had risen to 544 shillings. Over £ 50 had been gathered by the end of July and, at the completion of Volume III, nearly £ 100 had accumulated in the Propagandist Fund. Many contributions had been more than a shilling, of course, but Holyoake was especially gratified to have received some financial support from over three hundred individuals. There probably was no single motive which inspired this support. Many of those who gave very likely did so because they knew Holyoake, admired his courage and realized that his livelihood depended upon the meager remuneration he allowed himself as editor. For the immediate future, the *Reasoner* was secure. In November, Holyoake announced happily that "indirectly, covertly, insidiously, many papers attack religion, but only the *Reasoner* assails it openly and avowedly."[13]

The *Reasoner* was sustained not only by financial contributions but also because Holyoake had very able editorial assistance. When Holyoake was out of London lecturing—an activity which demanded an increasing amount of his time—or incapacitated by illness, he usually left management to William Chilton. T.W. Thornton, who contributed a number of well written articles on European socialism, also supervised the *Reasoner* in Holyoake's absence. In October 1847 for example, when Holyoake was "seized with an acute inflammation of the eye, which entirely deprived him of sight," Thornton came to the editorial rescue.[14] William Ashurst, Owen's solicitor, was so impressed by Holyoake's defense of free expression that he made substantial contributions and also wrote for the *Reasoner* under the pseudonym, "Edward Search." W.J.Birch, who had sustained the *Oracle of Reason*, was another upon whom

Holyoake came to depend. Most radical journals were the expression of one man. The *Reasoner*, however, might well be considered a cooperative production because Holyoake would have been unable to continue had it not been for the generosity of his associates.

Although circulation had increased only slightly, the *Reasoner* did not completely escape notice. The London *Daily News*, in a feature on the literature of the lower orders, patronizingly complimented both journal and editor:

> It is written with considerable ability, and for its avowed object—the dissemination of infidelity—conducted with no small amount of tact. It addresses itself to that large and constantly increasing class in English society—the class of artisans and others who have some native intelligence, and just enough of education to require a reason for their beliefs and opinions, but who have not enjoyed the close and consecutive education which is necessary to enable one to follow up a chain of argumentation; men, who in the awakening of consciousness of their own intelligence, are disposed to deny authority of tradition—who demand to be dealt with logically, and who are yet incompetent to use its higher formula.[15]

Holyoake was obviously pleased with these comments although he did not appreciate the analysis of his reading public, most of whom, he claimed, were "quite familiar with the higher forms of reasoning." As this article indicates, Victorians were becoming interested in the ideas and condition of the working classes. There were indeed two nations and the one was becoming very much aware that it knew little about what the men of factory and mill thought and to what goals they aspired.

As concerned as he was with progress, Holyoake possessed no romantic illusions about the general attitude of the lower orders toward reformers. Apathy, ingratitude and hostility more often than not were the prizes which the working class awarded to its leaders and educators. Those who would reform or widen the bounds of political liberty, Holyoake realized, not only required the support of a committed following, but they also must work in concert with one another.[16] Lacking this stable direction, the working classes would never achieve political, social or spiritual liberation. As Europe entered the year of revolutions which would create shock waves across the English Channel, the British working class found its leadership seriously fragmented.

Several weeks before the February revolution in France had begun, T.W. Thornton, reporting on the "banquet" activity in the *Reasoner*, stressed that political liberty was not the only objective of those who sought radical change in French society.[17] During the first weeks of the revolution, the London radicals could scarcely display enough enthusiasm for the French. At a meeting on March 5, the members of the John Street Institution adopted a laudatory "Address to the French People" to which Henry Hetherington vowed to affix 100,000 signatures.[18] Four days later, W.J. Linton and C.D. Collet, deputized by the London Chartists to visit Paris, reported their observations to a large crowd gathered at John Street. A "Democratic Committee of Observation on the French Revolution," which included many Chartists—Hetherington, Thomas Cooper, Linton, Collet, Bronterre O'Brien, James Watson and Holyoake— was organized. Their first act was the presentation of a new "People's Charter." Similar in tone to Lovett's charter of a dozen years earlier and addressed to the "Unrepresented Classes of Great Britain and Ireland," the petition announced that "We are not rioters," but "we demand our political rights."[19] These Chartists who frequently met at the John Street Institution did not follow the example of the French by expressing desire for sweeping social change. Uppermost in their minds was universal manhood suffrage and it soon became very clear that these men were not prepared to engage in any activity which might be construed as being conspiratorial. Elsewhere, Chartism appeared less moderate.

The potency of Chartism in 1848 is not really difficult to determine. Nearly destroyed by suppression in 1840, Chartism revived in the depression of the early 1840s and after the release of its leading agitators from prison. On May 2, 1842, the Charter, bearing over three million signatures, was again presented to Parliament. Not only did this petition contain 160% more names than did that of 1839, but it also revealed that working class support for the Charter had geographically become more widely distributed. When the depression reached its nadir in August 1842, a number of ill-timed strikes had taken place. Hoping to turn these economic protests to political advantage, Feargus O'Connor and the National Chartist Association pleaded with the strikers to stay out. All points of the Charter could be won, promised O'Connor, if the workers refused to return to their jobs.

Within a month, however, the great majority of strikes had been broken and the Chartist leaders were again faced with prosecution for their role in stirring up trouble. His prestige enhanced by a brilliant self-defense and acquittal, O'Connor was now able to dominate the National Chartist Association. His success, however, led to the eventual disintegration of Chartism. Although O'Connor was truly a man of the people and motivated by sincere convictions, he also was, in Holyoake's words, "a man of colossal incoherence."[20] The result was defection. William Lovett broke with O'Connor because of a disagreement over qualification for membership in the London Working Men's Association. When James Bronterre O'Brien criticized O'Connor's Land Scheme, he was vehemently denounced. Thomas Cooper, who had once been so active in Leicester Chartism and who had been imprisoned for his advocacy of the Charter, also parted company with O'Connor. In Glasgow, had it not been for O'Connor's hold over the rank and file, the local leadership might have deserted.[21]

In 1847 O'Connor was at the peak of his personal power and popularity. When he and nine other candidates who supported the Charter were elected to Parliament in August 1847, Chartist hopes increased that their goals might soon be attained. Crop failures in 1847, rising prices and news of continental revolutions catalyzed their enthusiasm. This exuberance must not be equated with unity. In early April 1848, O'Connor called a convention in London which was boycotted by the "moral force" Chartists. The day of April 10 was designated by the militants for a mass meeting in Kennington Common and the presentation of a last great petition to Parliament. If no real threat of revolution existed, there was, nevertheless, the distinct possibility of violence.

On the eve of the demonstration, Holyoake delivered an address at the John Street Institution entitled "The Chance for Obtaining an English Republic by Moral Means" in which he stressed the importance of opinion and reason in obtaining political and economic rights.[22] He did not participate in the following day's activities but went as a reporter to observe. The tale of the Chartist humiliation is well known; the great crowd did not materialize and the procession to Parliament consisted of three cabs instead of surging thousands. In the evening, the moderates gathered at the John Street Institution and founded the People's Charter Union. With Lovett, Hetherington, Watson and Collet, Holyoake was elected to the council of the Union. To disassociate completely the political demands of the Charter from revolutionary rhetoric was their basic intention. Many also believed that middle class support, within and outside of Parliament, should be sought. [23]

As far as Holyoake was concerned, the events of April 10 had confirmed his opinion that the weakness of working class political agitation resulted from a lack of unity among the leadership. A sense of fraternity and solidarity among Chartists had been lacking for years. They, too, like the Socialists, now had a calamity to recall. With the *Reasoner* temporarily solvent and capable editorial assistance available, Holyoake decided that he would make an extended lecture tour. His task, as he conceived it, was "to collect and organize the scattered friends of progress of former days, to suggest great practicable objects for them." [24] From this time, Holyoake became less insistent that religion was the *bête noire* of the laboring class. This important advance in his intellectual development was prompted of course by his observation of the Chartists in 1848 and by his earlier experience with Socialism. If progress were to be achieved, unity must be found first.

Holyoake began in Padiham on June 11 and did not complete his tour until October 13, 1848. After Padiham, he visited Accrington, Burnley, Oldham, Ashton-under-Lynn, Stayleybridge and Huddersfield. Chilton seems to have arranged Holyoake's schedule and contacted men in each town who might publicize the lectures and secure a meeting hall. In July, Holyoake spoke first in Liverpool; then, he returned to Ashton on July 5, where, chiefly because he was a celebrated freethinker, he was challenged to a debate by Dr. Benjamin West. For two evenings before 1,000 people, according to Holyoake's estimate, the two men discussed the relative merits of Christianity and atheism. Although Holyoake was somewhat at a disadvantage on the speaker's platform because of a weak voice, his wit and quick responses prevented him from being overwhelmed by his more oratorically gifted opponent. The interest created among the working class by such encounters should not be underestimated. For the price of a penny or less, a man could be treated to three or four hours entertainment in which he became more absorbed as the combatants warmed to one another's jibes.

But Dr. West and Holyoake got on so cordially off the rostrum that the local press suspected that the two were merely staging a very profitable performance. This accusation was of course untrue. In his report to the *Reasoner*, Holyoake explained that now "infidel and Christian seemed better to respect the integrity of each other". [25]

This comment was probably occasioned by the personableness of West, but it is also an indication that Holyoake's own attitude toward religion and clergymen had begun to moderate. On this note, Holyoake continued his travels, returning to London in October where he was scheduled to conduct rhetoric classes at the London Mechanics' Institute.

While on tour, Holyoake's lecture topics ranged from Biblical criticism to Socialism, Chartism and utilitarian morality. He found his audiences to be generally receptive, but hardly were they eager to be proselytized by an atheist missionary. Holyoake now discovered first-hand that the advice given him years before by his friend in Edinburgh, Jeffrey, was completely true. Most people, complained Holyoake, had been so prejudiced against anyone who criticized Christianity that they could only be approached on neutral issues. No reformer can afford to alienate those to whom he addresses himself. "By speaking on *secular* subjects," Holyoake declared, "they may come to believe that we mean well on others. But I shall not succeed at present so much noise is being made about my speculative opinions."[26] Holyoake surely recognized that he was now vulnerable to the same accusation he had once directed at Owen: of failing to capitalize on logically demonstrable errors of Christian doctrines. He had come to recognize that social reconstruction involved much more than condemning the Scriptures. Holyoake also had become acquainted with a few Christians, like Ashurst, whom he considered to be friends of progress. More important, because Holyoake now believed that the ineffective leadership given the working class by both the Socialists and the Chartists was in part responsible for much working class frustration, he would never again charge Christianity alone with the failure of the lower orders to achieve dignity.

Holyoake's recognition of inadequate leadership, his Owenite heritage and his fascination with the abortive French revolution are reflected in the articles he wrote during the winter of 1849 for an ephemeral Chartist weekly, the *Spirit of the Age*. Begun in July 1848, the *Spirit of the Age* was edited for a short time by Holyoake after William Ashurst had rescued it from debt. Although the *Spirit* was soon discontinued, the articles were reprinted in the *Reasoner* in April 1849. The present system of competition, claimed Holyoake, had no regard for the distribution of wealth; furthermore, social harmony was impossible when the economic system was founded on the pursuit of individual interest. "Associationism," a term undoubtedly borrowed from Louis Blanc's *Organization du travail*, was the label under which Holyoake presented his suggestions for a more equitable method of production and distribution.

Holyoake did not, however, advocate the development of national workshops or cooperatives as Blanc had done. His main concern was with the security and quality of the working man's life. Readers were emphatically assured that "associationism" was unrelated to revolution or anarchism. "The standard of association is no red flag of mere revolt—no black flag of plunder."[27] No attack was made on property and Holyoake wrote nothing about organizing the lower orders against property holders. He simply advocated "a government which shall guarantee the means of subsistence to all *industrious* citizens" and urged that the unskilled be educated so that their productive potential might be released. The establishment of a minimum standard of living and positive action to reduce economic fluctuation were the twin bases of Holyoake's proposals. Immediate and dramatic economic readjustment which Owen and even O'Connor had sought was forsaken for gradual progress. Convinced that the working class preferred "destitution to restriction on Freedom," Holyoake offered no specific suggestions for economic reform. True improvement, he believed, would occur only if minimum standards of existence and education were nationally assured.[28]

These ideas were not novel but were in fact reminiscent of earlier critiques of liberal economics such as that rendered by the Swiss nobleman, Simonde de Sismondi, in his *Nouveaux principes d'economie politique* (1819). Even in the *Wealth of Nations*, Adam Smith had advocated some regulation of the economy to prevent monopolistic corruption of his system; he had also suggested that the universalization of education and the elimination of extreme poverty be a function of government. Holyoake made no reference whatsoever to religion. Once he had been of the opinion that it was religion which crushed the human spirit; but now he asserted that poverty itself was the villain. Where was the solution? Owen's schemes had failed; Chartism had been discredited; and atheism had not prospered during the eight years in which Holyoake had been associated with the movement. Challenged by the Owenites to make a positive contribution to progress, the atheists had failed to respond. At this point, Holyoake sought to direct the attention of the "friends of progress" once again to moderate political agitation. In June 1849 the *Reasoner* analyzed the factors which prevented the development of a British revolution. Revolutionary fervor, Holyoake alleged, was only created by intense ideological commitment and party allegiance. These qualifications had been conspicuously lacking among those who would fundamentally alter the structure of British society. Radicals worshipped individual freedom more than social readjustment, thereby lessening the potential for revolution; they also confused party discipline with personal tyranny.[29]

During the summer of 1849, Holyoake had more time to continue his speculations because he again fell ill. Because the cholera was ravaging London, Holyoake had his will drawn for the sake of Eleanor and the children. The document, which was not made public until his death, reveals that he allowed himself little time to dwell on the grimness of these months:

> If this epidemic takes me suddenly, I shall be obliged to apologise to my readers and friends for my abrupt and unceremonious departure. Yet, when I think of it, I am so busy that I really have not time to die. My duties and my studies so occupy me that I shall be obliged to treat the cholera with rudeness, as I shall be too much engaged to pay it any attention.[30]

He survived the plague, but others were not so fortunate. Henry Hetherington, aged 57, fell victim to the cholera and died on August 24. Before a company of 2,000 persons, Holyoake delivered the funeral oration for the man who had been one of the founders of Chartism.[31] In October, T.W. Thornton also died, further reducing the little circle on whom Holyoake had come to depend. Holyoake's reaction to these losses were expressed in a short pamphlet entitled *The Logic of Death,* which became quite popular; by 1851 over 16,000 copies had been sold. In contradistinction to Christian doctrines of guilt and judgment which made death abhorrent, Holyoake stated his belief that matter or nature was eternal and that death was part of the normal sequence of events, not to be feared by anyone who had lived in freedom.[32] Although Holyoake rejected all supernatural beliefs, he did not seem to be convinced that death was the end of existence. Such expressions were not uncharacteristic of Victorian scepticism. In 1873 for example, John Stuart Mill startled his agnostic friends with his essay, *Theism,* which indicated that even Mill held a hope for an existence beyond the grave.

As Holyoake's friends and colleagues fell before the cholera, it also appeared that the *Reasoner* would fall before its old nemesis

—debt. The shilling contributions had seriously declined. Rather than implore his readers for money again, Holyoake decided that the *Reasoner* should be discontinued. In late December 1849, he warned the subscribers of the *Reasoner*'s demise and thanked them for helping to furnish "a page in the history of the permanent development of independent opinion in this country." [33] Three and a half years of existence, after all, was not a bad record for a working class publication. On January 2, 1850, however, the *Reasoner* was resurrected. Several of the more prosperous freethinkers wanted the *Reasoner* continued, and they promised to subsidize publication. Ten shillings a week for the next volume were guaranteed by W.J. Birch. This sum was matched by an anonymous donor. Arthur Trevelyan, a moderate Chartist, and other members of the John Street Institution also promised financial aid to the *Reasoner,* the price of which was now reduced to a penny in hopes that circulation could be increased. Holyoake once again had his journal rescued, but his benefactors did make Holyoake agree to one important condition. He was no longer to have unrestricted editorial freedom. Politics and social commentary were not to intrude upon the *Reasoner*'s pages; it was to be strictly a journal of atheism and free thought.

Why should a stipulation such as this have been made on the *Reasoner*? Freethinkers, like Christians, were becoming increasingly aware that their message was going unheeded by the laboring classes. The Christian reaction was either to preach the Word with renewed vigor hoping that working men might be awakened or to demonstrate the compatibility of Christianity with the social and political aspirations of the laboring class. Freethinkers, since the mid-eighteenth century, had been identifying rationalism with the most immediate problems of man—power and happiness. Now they desired to purge free thought of its worldly concerns. At this juncture in his career, G.J. Holyoake had no choice but to surrender to his friends' desires. "The reformation of theology" now became the *Reasoner*'s singular objective. [34] Ostensibly, Holyoake was willing to accept this complete reversal of his past editorial policy. "Communism and Republicanism," he wrote, "are now divorced from our pages, at which we are glad, because we cannot say these subjects are essentially atheistic."[35] Only in its earliest days, however, had the *Reasoner* been Communist and never did it advocate the dissolution of the British monarchy. The *Reasoner* had opened its columns to Chartists, Socialists, and revolutionaries, but now it would be unavailable to those who wished to contribute to the secular advancement of the working class. If atheism were the *Reasoner*'s only concern, he recognized that it would soon be read only by a dwindling sect. Holyoake must have been displeased but he did not choose to resign from his post.

During 1850 the *Reasoner* dealt almost exclusively with theological criticism, and like many periodicals at this time, it was vigorously anti-Catholic. In March 1850, however, Holyoake joined the staff of the *Leader* newspaper in addition to editing the *Reasoner*. Thornton Hunt, son of the poet, Leigh Hunt, and George Henry Lewes whom Holyoake called "intellectually the bravest man I have known," decided to found a radical weekly newspaper which would fill a journalistic gap between the quarterly reviews and the daily press.[36] Politics, economics and religion would all be treated critically. Both Hunt and Lewes were radicals with several years of personal experience in journalism, but they sought an efficient manager for their new venture. Ashurst recommended Holyoake to them because he knew how economy-minded Holyoake was. In addition to supervising the *Leader*'s finances, Holyoake's new position enabled him to continue writing on political issues. In the summer of 1850, for example, he contributed a series on association-ism, receiving enthusiastic cooperation from Louis Blanc.[37] Holy-oake could not have devoted much time to the *Leader* because of his other activities; nevertheless, his services were satisfactory to Hunt and Lewes. Most important, Holyoake was drawn into a much wider circle of associates.

With the *Leader* as a forum for his non-theological opinions, and with the financial stability of the *Reasoner* assured, Holyoake set about planning his lecture schedule for the summer of 1850. The list of topics he offered is another indication that his interest in social and political issues was not diminished by the conditions imposed on the *Reasoner*. Of eighteen advertised lectures, only eight were concerned with religion. Secular education, abolition of the newspaper stamp tax, Communism, universal suffrage, drama and literature were other topics about which Holyoake was prepared to speak or debate.[38] Although his tour, begun in the late spring, was shortened on doctor's advice, Holyoake found it rewarding. He began in Bradford, April 22 to 25, with four nights of religious discussion with a Mr. John Bowes. Each evening, the Temperance Hall, seating 1,500 people, was filled to capacity, some people paying as much as three pence for seats close to the platform.[39] Holyoake remained in Bradford to lecture to a large group of working men on April 30 and May 1. From there he journeyed to Keighley, Bingley, Heckmondwicke and Newcastle before being forced to cancel further engagements. The crowds of people who attended his lectures demonstrated that the apathy which had engulfed the working class in 1848 and 1849 was dissipating.

By the end of the summer, the *Reasoner* had achieved a circulation of nearly 2,000 per week. This was almost double the previous figures and seemed to testify to the value of undiluted theological criticism. Actually, the real causes of the *Reasoner*'s increased popularity were improving economic conditions and the reduction of its price to a penny. Among working class journalists it was an axiom that no weekly periodical priced at more than one penny could hope to succeed. Because of the increased circulation, Holyoake believed that he could regain his editorial independence. The *Reasoner*, he demanded, should return to "popular subjects while popular interest lasts."[40] Sustained enthusiasm was something which Holyoake had rarely known. Therefore, he wished to take every advantage of immediate popularity to spread his message; for Holyoake, irreligion was but one part of the gospel. Now, without actually including discursive articles on "popular subjects," Holyoake began to report his own activities in much more detail, a convenient technique for including political material.

In September he was elected President of the John Street Institution, an indication that he was gaining influence and respect. On October 6, he presided over the founding of the National Charter and Social Reform Union—another association of moderate Chartists and old Socialists who desired "to organize a movement of the people in order to obtain the enactment of the measures herein demanded, thereby securing for Great Britain and Ireland a just, wise and good government and such an equitable distribution of the fruits of industry as may be conducive to the best interests of all members of the commonwealth."[41] A national educational system, unstamped newspapers, and equitable taxation were among the specific reforms sought by this society. Although the Union accomplished virtually nothing, its existence did effect a formal tie between the two great organizations of the 1840s which had nearly passed into oblivion.

The National Chartist Association still existed but the leadership had no following of any consequence. In December 1850 Holyoake with G.J. Harney, Ernest Jones, and Feargus O'Connor was elected to the National Chartist Executive Committee. The reason for his association with these old-line Chartists became clear in January 1850 when he tried to encourage a greater "recognition of social rights" in their program. For the fruitless controversy which his advice generated, Holyoake had no enthusiasm. Soon after, he complained it was because of the actions of O'Connor and others that the reputation of Chartism had fallen "so low that no one cares to attempt to raise it."[42] But desire for social and political reform did exist in 1850, and for the next decade and a half, working class politics focused on attempts to stimulate popular interest in reform and to translate it into effective pressure upon the government.

Intending to make up the lectures lost because of his illness during the previous summer, Holyoake in February 1851 scheduled meetings in Nottingham, Newcastle and Glasgow. He again found his audiences most receptive. Reaction from local newspapers, which Holyoake always republished in the *Reasoner,* ranged from that of the *Newcastle Chronicle,* which considered Holyoake's meetings "disloyal or wicked" affairs where the "most violent sayings are applauded," to the *Nottingham Mercury* which reported that Holyoake was a "sharp thinker if not a particularly eloquent man."[43]   Although he no longer presented himself as an advocate of atheism, an increasing number of Christians began to consider the connection which existed between Holyoake's irreligion and his appeal to the working classes. He did not present his audiences with abstruse Biblical criticism as did most freethinkers, but he did tell them that Christianity was at best irrelevant to their needs and at worst a cruel delusion. For example, the *Ayr Observer* noted that Holyoake found his "patrons among the poor classes to whose poverty he appeals as argument for embracing his creed." There could be but one result if church and government ignored the condition of the people. Was it not, the *Observer* asked, an "unvarying rule to find principles of false religion hand in hand with principles of revolutionary politics?"[44] Holyoake was no revolutionary and it was not false religion, but irreligion, that he preached. Victorian Christians were becoming aware that few among the poor had contact with the church or chapel, and some had even come to believe that the improvement of the social and physical conditions of people was among the tasks of the church.

The most significant attempt to regain the working classes for Christianity was that made by the Christian Socialists. F.D. Maurice, Professor of Divinity at King's College, vicar Charles

Kingsley and the young socialist, John Malcolm Ludlow, had been drawn together by the events of April 1848. Fear of revolution, sympathy for the lower orders and a common desire to see the revitalization of Christianity in materialistic England motivated these three men to act. It was from *Politics for the People,* a series of tracts issued in 1848 which proclaimed harmony between Christianity and "liberty, equality, and fraternity," that Christian Socialism was created. In June 1850 Ludlow led the small circle of Christian Socialists in founding the Society for Promoting Working Men's Associations and proceeded to gather funds which might be lent to working men for the purpose of creating cooperative associations. Like Holyoake, Ludlow had learned of Associationism from his French contacts. When Edward Vansittart Neale, a man thoroughly acquainted with both English and French cooperative experiments, was elected to head the SPWMA, the Christian Socialist Movement spread rapidly. Not only did Neale invigorate the cause with his enthusiasm but also with £ 60,000 which he put at the disposal of the society.[45]

For several years, Ludlow had wanted to publish a weekly paper in which the compatibility of Christianity and Socialism would be demonstrated. On November 2, 1850, the first number of the *Christian Socialist* appeared. "Every Socialist system which has maintained itself for any time has endeavored to stand, or unconsciously to itself has stood upon those moral grounds of righteousness, self-sacrifice, mutual affection, common brotherhood, which Christianity vindicates to itself for an everlasting heritage," proclaimed the leader.[46] Why then are so few Christians found among the Socialists and so few Socialists among Christians? F.D. Maurice provided the answer to Ludlow. The anit-Christian sentiments so prevalent among the working classes had been instilled by atheists from Paine to Owen. Maurice was convinced that this tradition, now continued by Holyoake and the *Reasoner* must be combatted. The *Christian Socialist*'s first task was to join battle with the atheistic socialists.

Writing under the pseudonym "Parson Lot," Charles Kingsley addressed those who thought themselves "enlightened and rational." Specifically referring to Holyoake's activities, Kingsley wrote, "You have, many of you, been told and told till you believe it, that the Bible is the book which, above all others, supports priestcraft, superstition, and tyranny." Now it would be demonstrated that Scripture presented a God of love, a God who could intervene in human affairs and "break the laws of nature" if

necessary to interfere in the "People's cause."[47] If Kingsley was
hoping to provoke Holyoake, he failed. The *Reasoner* recommended
that freethinking socialists cooperate with the Christian Socialists.
"Open your halls to them," Holyoake advised. If and when progress
was achieved by socialists together, then theological disagreements
could be raised. Almost as an afterthought, Holyoake chided the
Christian Socialists for identifying socialism with Christianity; were
they really not trying to mask the shortcomings of their religion with
a socialist facade?[48]

Holyoake's temperate attitude only infuriated Maurice.
"Holyoake has declared war," he wrote to Kingsley in January
1851.[49] Ludlow and Kingsley, therefore, tried even harder to engage
Holyoake in a journalistic conflict. Each early number of their paper
reasserted that the most notable of human sentiments were common
to both Christianity and socialism. In Scripture, Ludlow claimed, the
dignity of the most menial labor was revealed. Especially designed to
challenge Holyoake and all other freethinkers was Ludlow's
assertion that God's actions were beyond the understanding and
ethics of men. Atheists and indeed most Victorian doubters had
usually begun with those passages in the Old Testament where
God's chosen people committed the most diabolical and vengeful
acts in His name. In debates with Christian opponents, the last
redoubt of the freethinker was invariably the Old Testament portrait
of God. Certainly Holyoake would respond. Then, believed Ludlow,
Christianity would sweep away the "every-man-his-own-God-
destroyer-gospel of the *Reasoner*."[50] Holyoake, however, was
resolute in his decision not to become embroiled in useless
theological controversy with the Christian Socialists. Ludlow and
Kingsley, during the spring of 1851, finally relinquished attempts to
irritate Holyoake and used their journal for advertising the
SPWMA.

For not putting these Christians in their place, Holyoake earned
considerable criticism from his fellow freethinkers. Although he had
perceived the challenge, Holyoake preferred not to respond to the
Christian Socialists because, as he later explained,

> the sole end of public controversy is not private
> gratification or party victory, but the public good.
> In this case the public might regard it as a scandal
> that two societies, having the same social end in
> view, should appear as the opponents of each
> other. [51]

The attack by Ludlow and Maurice was the first real test of Holyoake's conclusion that theological haggling was of no value to workingmen. Holyoake persisted so resolutely in this conviction that he refused to lecture on both Socialism and theology in the same town during any one engagement. Religious debates and controversies created sensations in Victorian England and Holyoake might easily have turned notoriety to profit. But the unification of old and new "friends of progress" remained his sole objective; all other activity was an unwelcome distraction.

From May to October 1851, Holyoake again was traveling and lecturing. The *Reasoner* is filled with reports of the lectures, the receptions given and the response which was provoked. The first two weeks in May, Holyoake spent in Glasgow, Paisley and Dundee. On May 16 he spoke of the benefits of national education to a public meeting in Galashiels; on May 20 he was at Carlisle; from there he journeyed to Lancaster where he was engaged until May 23. By October, Holyoake had visited Newcastle, Whitehaven, Edinburgh, Padiham, Colne, Burnley, Todmorden, South Shields, Stockton-on-Tees, Miles Platting, Preston and Manchester. Not only were his audiences very enthusiastic, but Holyoake also began to discern a renewed interest in organizing. From Leicester, for example, he received word that "some of the old Socialists, with a few of the new ones—initiated into the movement by more modern freethinkers— have signified a desire to mutually and systematically bring to bear their means upon some of the evils of the time."[52] The possibility of coordinated activity was clearly present.

When he returned to London, Holyoake found that the beginning of a society had already been made. The London City Mission and a group of Christians who called themselves the Victoria Park Mission, taking special note of the London Free-thinkers, had been challenging them and preaching against infidelity at outdoor meetings. Members of the John Street Institution were described by these evangelists as "democratic socialists who mixed infidelity with their politics so that a Christian's blood runs cold."[53] Most "democratic socialists" and freethinkers were not content to remain silent when criticized by Christians. On Monday, November 24, 1851, three hundred freethinkers gathered at the City Road Hall of Science in London. Thornton Hunt presided and Holyoake, who apparently had nothing to do with calling the meeting, delivered a brief address in which he complimented their initiative and requested that questions of politics and socialism be given a place equal to infidelity. [54] Most encouraging for Holyoake personally was the title adopted, the Society of Reasoners. They also chose as their philosophical platform, his article, "Truths to Teach," which he had recently written as a preface to the twelfth volume of the *Reasoner* (Appendix 2). In that piece, Holyoake summarized the major tasks of contemporary free thought: it should be taught that knowledge which results from experienced phenomena only can be trusted; and opinions which could be demolished by reason and free discussion must be discarded. [55] Rather than present policy directives, Holyoake sought to provide a widely acceptable and practical philosophy within which men might work most effectively for their intellectual and social advancement. Since Paine's *Age of Reason,* British freethinkers had actually been telling men what not to believe; Holyoake had great hopes that freethinkers would now begin to provide positive and constructive ideas.

Almost immediately, the Society of Reasoners altered its name to the Secular Society. "Secular" was a term which had been suggested to Holyoake some months before by William Ashurst as being more appropriate than "atheist" because it was devoid of negative connotations.[56] Holyoake was very pleased with this term and simply defined "secular" as the antonym of "sacred." On December 29, 1851, the Secular Society sponsored a Free Discussion Festival and tea at which Holyoake presented the main address. It was necessary, he believed, for freethinkers to differentiate themselves from those who appeared to be irreligious because of dissolute lives. He meant that freethinkers should observe conventional standards of morality; laziness, drunkenness and frivolity were not to be characteristics of freethinkers. By no means, however, were freethinkers to be conformists. Their intellectual independence was to be asserted by a definition of principles and objectives. He encouraged those present to create an organization and invited all who agreed with "Truths to Teach" to form Secular Societies and communicate with him, the Secretary of the Central Secular Society. [57]

Not everyone at this festival unreservedly accepted Holyoake's leadership. After addresses by Holyoake, W.J. Birch, and James Watson, Robert Cooper, a frequent and very popular lecturer on atheism, asked to be heard. Free thought, Cooper warned, was becoming too conservative; Holyoake's counsel was too careful and was incompatible with that policy which he preferred—a frontal assault on Christianity. Cooper, like Holyoake, had been an Owenite missionary and a militant atheist as well. Afraid at one time that the Christian Socialists were endangering progress, Cooper had written to Holyoake, "I boldly affirm that the greatest impediment to socialism is priestcraft....We must fight to expose it and destroy it by meeting it boldly, fearlessly, resolutely."[58] Because he had not vigorously replied to the *Christian Socialist,* declared Cooper, Holyoake had done great harm to the cause and reputation of free thought. To these criticisms, which seem to have been given quite unexpectedly, Holyoake replied that he was by no means a conservative; if freethinkers really desired to be effective, they should act cautiously and not emulate the Chartists who "were so eager to bite, that they did not always wait to find a clear place for their teeth."[59] Because the *Reasoner* was the sole organ of British free thought, Holyoake assured Cooper that his opinions would be published if he cared to submit them.

The Secular Society met again on January 29, 1852, to celebrate the birth of Tom Paine and again on March 29. The *Reasoner,* however, gave the society very little notice, an indication that Holyoake was not especially excited about the organization. This observation is reinforced by several warnings that an organization could be a hindrance as well as an aid to progress. There are, Holyoake wrote, "well intending reformers who believed that no progress is made unless disgust and execration be awakened. This we respectfully believe is altogether erroneous. Disgust must be excited against error—to excite it against ourselves is simply suicidal."[60] Intended for Robert Cooper, and for anyone of an especially zealous nature, these words might well have been written about Holyoake by Owen a dozen years before. In 1846, Holyoake had attempted to found a society for the propagation of free thought. With another opportunity open to him now, he appeared to balk, afraid that a society might do more harm than good for the cause of working class progress. Such apprehension was not, however, the only reason why he failed to become more deeply involved with Secularism at this time. In January 1852 his services were requested by the radical National Parliamentary and Financial Reform Association for a rather special mission.

Created in 1849 by Francis Place, the National Parliamentary and Financial Reform Association sought franchise reform as a prerequisite to control over government expenditure.[61] More control over the budget was desired by radicals and Manchester liberals alike. John Bright, Richard Cobden and Joseph Hume, who had several times presented a "Little Charter" in the House of Commons, had also been trying to construct a capital-labor alliance. Now they threw their support to Place's association. Sir Joshua Walmsley, M.P. from Leicester and advocate of the Chartist cause, was elected President. It if were to succeed, the executive council of the Association believed that the support of the Chartist leaders was essential. To this end, numerous meetings were held between 1849 and 1852. The Association, dominated by middle class radicals, refused to go further for franchise reform than to demand household suffrage. Moderate Chartists, including Holyoake who applauded the Association in the *Leader,* believed this resolve enough to warrant Chartist support. Even Feargus O'Connor had become convinced that an alliance on this basis was warranted; but other Chartists, led by G.J. Harney and Ernest Jones, refused to depart from their commitment to universal suffrage. They accused the parliamentary radicals of seeking only the political advantage which they could gain from working class support. Furthermore, this issue irreparably divided the Chartists because Harney and Jones broke with O'Connor and formed their own executive committee.

One last attempt was made in early 1852 by the Association to create the alliance. In January, Holyoake was informed that he had been elected to the board of the Association. First, he was invited to participate in the planning of a conference to be held on March 2 and 3. Hopefully, he would be able to convince the more stubborn Chartists to concede the point of universal suffrage and to support the National Reform Association. In a letter to Thornton Hunt, Walmsley expressed his great respect for Holyoake's judgment and indicated his belief that Holyoake's moderating influence might well be significant at the forthcoming conference.[62] The conference began painfully for those who desired a meeting of minds. Walmsley's opening address was followed by Ernes Jones' denunciation of the agenda.[63] On the second day, Hume presided over the franchise debate. A motion was, of course, presented for manhood suffrage and Holyoake rose to reply. He accused Jones and his friends of purposely making a division in the conference by introducing a resolution which was known to be unacceptable to the middle class radicals. If the Chartists were so democratic, Holyoake retorted, why did they not include women's suffrage in their amendment? If they did not, they were no better than those who stood fast, at this time, for household suffrage.[64]

Convinced that household suffrage was as much as could immediately be obtained, Holyoake implored the Chartists to cooperate with the radicals. Unless, he advised, we distinguish "between what is right and what is possible, we shall flounder forever, talking grandly and patriotically of the possibly right, and perpetuating year after year, the full measure of practical wrong."[65] The conference adjourned in discord. After March 1852 the National Parliamentary and Financial Reform Association no longer functioned. Firmly entrenched radicals like Walmsley were returned to Parliament in the following general election but did not owe their victory either to the Association or to Chartist endorsement. In Frances Gillespie's opinion, the diverse objectives of middle and working classes fostered a suspicion which corrupted every attempt at political cooperation.[66] The demise of the Association presented Holyoake with another instance of working class radicals sabotaging piecemeal progress when they realized that their ultimate objectives could not be immediately achieved. Who could tell what had been sacrificed on the altar of universal suffrage? Chartism, after this failure to evolve into a union with parliamentary radicalism, finally came to an end. Holyoake now returned to lecturing and to Secularism even more wary than before of trying to create an organization of men who, like the Chartists, had so frequently demonstrated their lack of ability to recognize the necessity of compromise.

In April 1852 Robert Cooper's reports began to appear in the *Reasoner*. Holyoake's journal, Cooper complained, lacked enthusiasm. Freethinkers wanted "heart as well as mind." To illustrate, Cooper described his recent activity in Nottingham where he had touched his audiences with florid oratory. Tyranny and priestcraft, he proclaimed, were now mustering "every engine of darkness and crime" to crush political and intellectual liberty. "Organization," he concluded, "is at this moment, our urgent necessity."[67] Further communication during May and June told of Cooper's activities in Derby, Dewesbury, Heckmondwicke, Bradford, Blackburn, Stockport and Manchester. Everywhere, he testified, workingmen were pressing for an organization to combat the "vulture oppression."[68] Cooper's emotionalism was repugnant to Holyoake. With Secular societies being demanded and, in some cases, on the verge of being created, Holyoake recognized that he must play a more active role in the movement if moderation were to have a voice.

Accordingly, after lecturing to the newly formed Bradford Secular

Society on May 7, Holyoake journeyed to Manchester to attend an *ad hoc* conference of freethinkers. Men from thirteen towns gathered there, on May 9, to consider what might be gained by coordinated activity. Holyoake presented a resolution which was adopted calling upon each representative to return to his town, insure that a society secretary was appointed, communicate progress to the *Reasoner,* and finally prepare for a general conference in Manchester.[69] During the remainder of May, Holyoake lectured almost daily. On the 16th, he spoke at the Finsbury Institution in London on the "Despotism of Reformers"; on May 17 and 18, he held a discussion in Northampton; on the 19th, he was in Leicester. Holyoake returned to the John Street Institution on May 23 and 24 to speak on the "Positive Principles of Free Enquiry"; then it was back to Leicester on the 25th. This very strenuous schedule was maintained for most of the summer, with the exception of early August when he was forced to take a week's rest.

Amid this period of great activity, Holyoake celebrated the completion of the *Reasoner*'s twelfth volume. No such journal had ever been sustained for so long. Because he did not indulge in sensationalism and emotionalism, Holyoake acknowledged that the *Reasoner* would never, in the future, as it seldom had in the past, pay for itself. But he vowed to continue his policy of appealing to "just and deep feelings" with the unadorned truth rather than creating false enthusiasm by using "passionate phrases, moon stricken tales, patriotic invective, and spicy reports."[70] As a freethinker, he would continue to criticize only those facets of religion which inhibited social progress.

Holyoake also encouraged his readers to support that political party which seemed most concerned with extending social and political rights.[71] At this point, Holyoake committed a tactical error for he raised grave doubts about his integrity by advocating support of the Whigs. Although the *Reasoner* endorsed J.A. Roebuck—a man who hated the Whigs—for Parliament, Holyoake wrote,

> A Whig is to be preferred to a Tory. True, a Whig is but the mitigated form of Tory; but though the Whig may not be more liberal than a Tory (which he, on the whole, always is) he is to be preferred because he professes *liberality,* and the profession of it is an advantage. It makes liberality fashionable, and encourages the imitation of it and at last the real thing springs up. The Whigs made freedom possible among us.[72]

To most of the *Reasoner*'s readers—working class or middle class radicals—such reasoning was indeed curious. In praising the Whigs was not Holyoake really a traitor to the working class? Some were persuaded that Holyoake had abandoned the radical political tradition which Owenism, Chartism and free thought each had been carrying on for years. Of course, his commendation of the Whigs was highly qualified, but suspicions of Holyoake's growing conservatism were hardly dispelled by it. Always concerned about freethinkers exciting an undesirable reaction among Christians, Holyoake had apparently forgotten that radicals could also become very disturbed. No doubt, Holyoake had to make considerable explanation of these remarks in his travels during the summer of 1852.

By the end of September, he had been to Dudley, Stourbridge, Kingswinford, Stafford, Newcastle-on-Tyne, Middlesborough, Keighley and Little Bolton. Secularist organization had also proceeded apace even though there is little evidence that Holyoake was an active promoter. On August 28 and 29, Holyoake attended another conference in Manchester. October 3, 1852, was designated as the day when the general conference of Secularists would be held. Each incipient society was invited to send one delegate for each forty members or fraction thereof; these representatives were to report the size, activities and potential for growth of their society. In response to a query from the Sheffield Rational Society, Holyoake stated that the name of the society was of no consequence. Furthermore, Holyoake promised that local constitutions and management would be left unrestricted by any association which this conference might create.[73] The intention was to seek only that which might be gained by cooperation but not to circumscribe the activities of the individual society.

When the Secularists convened in Manchester on October 3, Holyoake took the chair and in his opening address to the delegates he alluded to his earlier attempts to organize freethinkers. For stimulating organization at this time, he gave credit to Robert Cooper, who for unexplained reasons, was not present. Holyoake's speech was not designed to promote enthusiasm for organizing. Indeed, he remarked, he was not convinced that "this shall prove the right time to commence."[74] After Holyoake finished, the delegates delivered their reports. Twenty-four societies were represented with Manchester, claiming seventy members, being the largest.[75] These accounts were brief and optimistic; by noon the delegates were ready to attend to the framing of a constitution. The document which their discussion produced was hardly a constitution in the strict sense of the word. It defined Secularism as "the philosophy of the things of time"; the principles and general objectives of Secularists, almost a paraphrase of Holyoake's principles, were also stated. Other than a clause encouraging local societies to establish Secular day and Sunday schools, absolute freedom was granted to choose "special work to be done in that neighborhood." Any group which agreed to the general principles had the right to be recognized as a secular society. Only two obligations were placed upon confederating societies; each was to submit dues of two shillings per year per member to a general "propagandist" fund, and each society was to send representatives to an annual conference. Before departing, the delegates agreed that Holyoake, Watson, Birch, Arthur Trevelyan and William Chilton would function in the capacity of a Central Council until the next annual conference. Holyoake's final instruction—an admonition that profitable confederacy required "independent, self-sustaining" societies—was intended to encourage Secularists to greater local effort and to leave them sceptical of any federative ambitions. [76]

In 1846 Holyoake had tried to build an organization and had not succeeded. Now, with the greatest reservations, he found himself at the head of a loose confederation of Secular societies. This was the first time that freethinkers had constructed anything resembling a national organization. Most of them were ex-Owenites and Secularism was thoroughly grounded in Owen's philosophy. They realized, however, that Owen's economics had been an inadequate response to the problems of the British working classes. Holyoake's real task, utilizing the philosophy and principles upon which all had agreed, was to direct the energy of these men in such a way that they could develop and carry out more appropriate solutions to problems with which both Owen and the Chartists had unsuccessfully grappled. Holyoake wanted the Secularists to continue the task of increasing the intellectual and economic capabilities of the laboring classes and of gaining for them a voice in British politics.

An equally difficult task would be that of preventing the energy which created Secularism from being dissipated in factional conflict. Holyoake had observed, too closely perhaps, the disintegration of both Owenism and Chartism. It seemed to him that internal weakness had brought both organizations to a dreary end. Now he faced the dilemma which neither Owen nor the Chartists had been able to solve. If the Secularists were a tightly disciplined party, the step from principles to action was an easy one. An imposed or false cohesion would, however, tend to provoke internal strife. On the other hand, a confederation which permitted free expression to dissident factions could accomplish little because it would be seriously handicapped by a lack of unity. Holyoake believed that strong local societies were the prerequisite of a potent national association. Realizing that he lacked the ability to dominate the total membership, Holyoake wished that a stronger base would be constructed from which a disciplined association might be voluntarily created. It was from those Secularists who desired immediate action and achievement, therefore, that Holyoake's greatest criticism came.

NOTES TO CHAPTER THREE

[1] Walter Houghton, *The Victorian Frame of Mind* (New Haven: Yale University Press, 1957). See especially chapters six and seven, pp. 137-160.

[2] R.K. Webb, *The British Working Class Reader, 1790-1848* (London: George Allen and Unwin, Ltd., 1955). Chapter one provides an especially fine description of the relationship between working class journalism, literacy, and the tastes of the reading public.

[3] Holyoake did keep a conventional diary, but the entries are so fragmentary as to make them of minimal value. See McCabe's comments, *Life and Letters of Holyoake*, I, 125.

[4] *Reasoner*, I, No. 1 (June 3, 1846), 1.

[5] *Ibid.*, No. 6 (July 8, 1846), 95.

[6] John Buxton to Holyoake (June 14, 1846), No. 168, C.U.

[7] See *Reasoner*, I, No. 6 (July 8, 1846), 80-88 and No. 7 (July 15, 1846), 102-105 for the details of these deliberations.

[8] *Ibid.*, I, No. 9 (July 29, 1846), 136.

[9] See Appendix I for Holyoake's complete financial report of the first twenty volumes of the *Reasoner*. The Propagandist fund, not begun until Volume III, must have been applied to the accumulated debt.

[10] *Reasoner*, I No. 19 (October 7, 1846), 249-51.

[11] *Ibid.*, II, No. 27 (December 2, 1846), 1-6 and No. 38 (February 17, 1846), 79.

[12] *Ibid.*, III, No. 53 (June 2, 1846), 298-302.

[13] *Ibid.*, II, Volume-Script (November 13, 1847).

[14] *Ibid.*, III, No. 72 (October 13, 1847), *Utilitarian Record*, 91.

[15] *Ibid.*, No. 76 (November 10, 1847), 611.

[16] *Ibid.*, No. 77 (November 17, 1847), 625-29.

[17] *Ibid.*, IV, No. 89 (February 9, 1848), 141-44.

[18] *Ibid.*, No. 93 (March 8, 1848), 197-200.

[19] *Ibid.*, No. 94 (March 22, 1848), 233-34.

[20] Holyoake, *Sixty Years*, I, 107.

[21] Alex Wilson, "Chartism in Glasgow," *Chartist Studies*, ed. Asa Briggs, p. 279. For a contemporary description of Chartist dissension see R.G. Gammage, *History of the Chartist Movement*, especially Ch. X.

[22] *Reasoner*, IV, No. 99 (1848), 282-85.

[23] Frances E. Gillespie, *Labor and Politics in England, 1850-1867* (Durham, N.C.: Duke University Press, 1927), p. 68.

[24] *Reasoner*, V, No. 111 (1848), 107.

[25] *Ibid.*, No. 113 (1848), 130.

[26] *Ibid.*, No. 122 (1848), 186.

[27] *Ibid.*, VI, No. 150 (1849), 227.

[28] *Ibid.*, No. 153 (1849), 273-76.

[29] *Ibid.*, No. 159 (1849), 369.

[30] McCabe, *Life and Letters of Holyoake*, I, 159.

[31] *Reasoner*, VII, No. 9 (1849), 129-33. Holyoake also wrote Hetherington's biography for the *Dictionary of National Biography*.

32 G.J. Holyoake, *The Logic of Death* (London: James Watson, 1850), p. 14.

33 *Reasoner*, VII, Introduction (c: December 19, 1849), vii; see also *Reasoner*, VII, No. 26 (1849), 393-96.

34 *Ibid.*, VIII, No. 2 (1850), 9.

35 *Ibid.*, No. 11 (1850), 89-90.

36 Anna Theresa Kitchel, *George Lewes and George Eliot* (New York: The John Day Company, 1933), pp. 63-89. See Holyoake, *Sixty Years*, I, 226-244 for his comments on Hunt, Lewes, and the *Leader*.

37 Lousi Blanc to Holyoake (August 21, 1850), No. 382, C.U.

38 *Reasoner*, IX, No. 3 (1850), 34-35.

39 *Ibid.*, No. 4 (1850), 50-53. Holyoake's estimate of the attendance is substantiated by a report from the *Bradford Observer* which he reprinted in the *Reasoner*.

40 *Ibid.*, No. 24 (1850), 277.

41 *Ibid.*, X, No. 2 (1850), 16. See also Gillespie, *Labor and Politics in England, 1850-1867*, p. 72.

42 *Reasoner*, X, No. 18 (1851), 310.

43 *Ibid.*, No. 32 (1851), 478; and No. 24 (1851), 376.

44 *Ibid.*, No. 3 (1850), 25-26.

45 Torban Christensen, "Origin and History of Christian Socialism," *Acta Theologica Danica*, III, 1962, provides the best account of Christian Socialism. Pages 142-161 are especially relevant to the history of the SPWMA and the *Christian Socialist*. C.E. Raven, *Christian Socialism, 1848-1854* (London: Macmillan and Co., Ltd., 1920) is very sympathetic but nevertheless accurate. For Neale's role, see Philip Backstrom, *Christian Socialism and Cooperation in Victorian England* (London: Croom Helm Ltd., 1974).

46 *Christian Socialist*, No. 1 (November 2, 1850), p. 1.

47 *Ibid.*, No. 2 (1850), p. 9 and No. 4 (1840), pp. 25-26.

48 *Reasoner*, X, No. 15 (1851), 265-66.

49 Frederick Maurice (ed.), *The Life of F.D. Maurice* (New York: Charles Scribner's Sons, 1884), II, 57.

50 *Christian Socialist*, No. 13 (January 25, 1851), pp. 97-98; No. 25 (February 8, 1851), pp. 113-14; and No. 17 (February 22, 1851), pp. 130-31.

51 *Reasoner*, XI, No. 13 (1851), 189.

52 *Ibid.*, X, No. 32 (1851), 475.

53 *Ibid.*, XI, No. 12 (1851), 178.

54 *Ibid.*, XII, No. 2 (1851), 17-20.

55 *Ibid.*, No. 1 (1851), 1. See Appendix II.

56 *Ibid.*, XI, No. 6 (1851), 87.

57 *Ibid.*, XII, No. 9 (1852), 129-31.

58 *Ibid.*, IX, No. 9 (1850), 103. Note: Cooper wrote these words before the appearance of the *Christian Socialist*.

59 *Ibid.*, XII, No. 9 (1852), 135.

60 *Ibid.*, No. 11 (1852), 161.

61 Gillespie, *Labor and Politics in England*, Chapter 3, pp. 77-109.

62 J. Walmsley to Thornton Hunt (February 22, 1852), No. 472, C.U.

63 *The Times* (London), March 3, 1852, p. 7.

64 *Ibid.*, March 4, 1852, p. 5.

65 *Reasoner*, XII, No. 17 (1852), 266.

66 Gillespie, *Labor and Politics in England*, p. 108.

67 *Reasoner*, XII, No. 21 (1852), 331-32.

68 *Ibid.*, No. 18 (1852), 444.

69 *Ibid.*, No. 26 (1852), 412.

70 *Ibid.*, No. 2 (1852), 17-21.

71 *Ibid.*, XIII, No. 1 (1852), 1-3.

72 *Ibid.*, XII, No. 3 (1852), 33.

73 *Ibid.*, XIII, No. 13 (1852), 206; No. 14 (1852), 221-22; and No. 15 (1852), 236.

74 *Ibid.*, No. 19 (1852), 298-93.

75 *Ibid.*, No. 20 (1852), 305-08. The societies represented were the following: Bolton, 27; Blackburn, 50; Bradford, 49; Burnley, 28; Bury*, 0; Glasgow, 50; Keighley, 12; Leigh, 16; Manchester, 70; Miles Platting, no figure; Newcastle-on-Tyne, 20; Nottingham, 31; Over Darwen, 4; Paisley, 50; Preston*, 20; Rochdale, 15; Stafford, no figure; Sheffield, 32; Stockport, 24; Tomorden*, no figure. Societies in London, Ashton-under-Lyne, Heywood, and Oldham did not submit reports.

76 *Ibid.*, No. 22 (1852), 353-356. Herein is recorded the "Constitution and Objects of Secular Societies" and Holyoake's concluding remarks to the conference. See Appendix III for selections from this document.

*Indicates report by letter only.

CHAPTER IV

SECULARISM

When J.B. Bury succeeded Lord Acton as the Regius Professor of Modern History at Cambridge in 1902, he stated in his inaugural lecture that history was "simply a science, no less and no more" and that it was an increasingly "powerful force for stripping the bandages of error from the eyes of men." [1] A decade later, Bury produced his short but immensely popular *History of the Freedom of Thought* in which Holyoake was described as one of the "most important English freethinkers who appealed to the masses." [2] In 1929 J.M. Robertson published his encyclopedic *History of Freethought in the Nineteenth Century* and also accorded a rather prominent place to Holyoake and the British Secularists. These historians were imbued with the nineteenth century vision of progress through science and reason; they believed that both they and the freethinkers of whom they wrote were continuing the great work of extinguishing superstition and ignorance.

Free thought is no longer a topic of such historical interest. One reason, of course, is that few twentieth century historians have been able to retain that older confidence in reason and the belief in progress. Also, factors other than the activity of freethinking intellectuals have been adduced as being responsible for the process of secularization in Western society. As church historian Martin E. Marty has written, it was not the freethinkers but simply "mundane pursuits" which made the church and religion increasingly irrelevant for all classes of Victorian society. [3] And it has been demonstrated that British atheists had as little success after mid-century in their attempts to gain converts as did any church or sect. [4] To be fully understood, however, Secularism must be studied in a context broader than free thought. It was indeed part of a larger process through which the working classes were becoming more integrated with the rest of Victorian society. The story of Secularism and of

Holyoake's role in that movement is only beginning to be adequately delineated.[5]

It is incorrect to make the unqualified claim that the Manchester conference was the beginning of organized British Secularism. Many of the delegates believed that they had created a federation of freethinking societies, but they and the several historians of British free thought and Secularism have held a somewhat erroneous opinion about the Manchester meeting. For example, J.M. Robertson assigned the convention an importance it did not have. Furthermore, he was misled into believing that Holyoake was its principal convener.[6] Recent studies, such as the analysis of British irreligion made by John Eros and David Tribe's monograph on the National Secular Society err by ascribing aspirations to Holyoake which the documents indicate that he did not possess.[7] In 1852 and consistently thereafter, Holyoake expressed the most ambiguous opinions about the usefulness of organized Secularism. To be sure, the British public came to associate Secularism with Holyoake's name more than it did with any other person because he produced so many articles, tracts, speeches and books on the subject. Careful reading of them, however, reveals that Holyoake was very hesitant about establishing an organization. For him, the Manchester conference affirmed a set of principles and did not initiate a national federation.

Holyoake had come to limit his definition of Secularism to a series of rational, common-sense postulates about the world and human behavior. Freethinkers had credited themselves, since the time of Voltaire, for liberating man from religious dogmas which alternately tormented and then soothed the mind. Although they had proved themselves capable of rendering criticism of religion, rationalists had found it difficult to refute the charge that they had failed to construct a more acceptable basis for morality. By compounding reason with simple utilitarian ethics, Holyoake hoped that Secularism would prove to be an acceptable substitute for Christianity. Secularism, claimed Holyoake, was the "province of the real, the known, the useful, and the affirmative. It is the practical side of scepticism. The Secularist . . . asks what will but conduce to the welfare of man in this world, and endeavors to promote that."[8] By itself this assertion was inadequate. So many schemes conducive to human welfare and progress had been formulated but as yet rationalists had been unable to develop a distinctive or systematized ideology. Even if he had possessed the genius to formulate a Secular philosophy, Holyoake did not have the credentials required to encourage many to adopt it.

At this very time, early 1853, Harriet Martineau completed her English abridgement of August Comte's *Cours de philosophie positive.* John Stuart Mill and a few others had already introduced positivist ideas into Britain, but Comte's remarkable system was presented in a form which could be comprehended only by men of rather exceptional education. Miss Martineau's translation made Comte's ideas available to a far greater number of people; indeed she has been credited with accomplishing more than anyone in Great Britain to promote understanding of Comte's theory of history, his hierarchy of the sciences and his optimistic conclusions about the scientific, or positive, method for rationally reconstructing society. No other thinker of the nineteenth century had his ideas so enthusiastically accepted by his contemporaries.[9]

Miss Martineau had good reasons for what must have been a most laborious task. "I believe," she wrote in the preface,

> no one can inquire into the mode of life of young
> men of the middle and operative classes without
> being struck with the desire that is shown, and the
> sacrifices that are made, to obtain the means of
> scientific study. That such a disposition would be
> baffled, and such study rendered almost ineffec-
> tual, by the desultory character of scientific exposi-
> tion in England, while such a work as Comte's was
> in existence, was not to be borne, if a year or two of
> humble toil could help, more or less, to supply the
> need.[10]

Accordingly, the first book of the two-volume abridgement was devoted to summarizing the Comtean description of the natural sciences. She claimed, however, a second and far more important justification for her efforts. Typically we find here the evangelist dwelling happily with the rationalist in a Victorian intellectual. Miss Martineau explained:

> The supreme dread of everyone who cares for the
> good of nation or race is that men should be adrift
> for want of an anchorage for their convictions. I
> believe that no one questions that a very large
> proportion of our people are now so adrift. With
> pain and fear, we see that a multitude, who might
> and should be among the wisest and best of our

> citizens are alienated for ever from the kind of faith
> which sufficed for all in an organic period which
> has passed away, while no one has presented to
> them, and they cannot obtain for themselves, any
> ground of conviction as firm and clear as that
> which sufficed for our fathers in their day. The
> moral dangers of such a state of fluctuation as has
> thus arisen are fearful in the extreme, whether the
> transition stage from one order of conviction to
> another be long or short. The work of M. Comte is
> unquestionably the greatest single effort that has
> been made to obviate this kind of danger . . .[11]

Comte's belief in progress and his passion for serving humanity had assuaged Miss Martineau's uneasiness over her inability to retain her religious heritage; she was thoroughly convinced that science had replaced both religion and metaphysics and that human progress was now a function of natural, discoverable axioms. Like evangelical Christians who often defended their faith on the grounds that it provided a sound foundation for life and morality, Miss Martineau rejoiced that her new religion, unburdened by mystery, could do as well.

Holyoake was greatly impressed. One of the first journals to review Miss Martineau's translation, he proclaimed, "The Secularists of England are hourly reproached with having no doctrine, no faith, no privilege to construct but only the power to destroy. This book may extinguish that reproach forever."[12] The *Positive Philosophy* became his "scientific bible of Secularism"; Volume XV of the *Reasoner* bore the subtitle, "Journal of Free Thought and Positive Philosophy." It is likely that Holyoake, who had only a smattering of French, had little or no previous contact with Comte's ideas. Nevertheless, he immediately recognized that an unmistakeable affinity existed between the positive philosophy and Secularism. Positivism and Secularism contended that Christianity and metaphysics were outmoded and unnecessary. "The Postive Philosophy is distinguished from the ancient . . . ," claimed Comte, "by nothing so much as its rejection of all inquiry into cause, first and final; and its confining research to the invariable relations which constitute natural laws."[13] Man was part of nature; therefore, nature's laws were applicable to human society. Comte and Holyoake both insisted that men were obliged to serve the cause of human happiness and progress. Morality was guaranteed by this imperative, by the basic benign nature of men and by their rationality. Unlike

Comte, Holyoake refused to turn humanity into an object of worship, but he did consider that the desire for human improvement motivated all honest reformers.

Comte's assumptions about behavior were not greatly different from Robert Owen's suppositions, but positivism did have a distinct appeal. Comte asserted not only that an exact science of society was possible but also that his knowledge was open to every man. The intellectual elitism which plagued Owen's philosophy was initially avoided by Comte who claimed that "the philosophic spirit is simply accessible to human reason."[14] This conviction was the essence of Secularism; their mechanics' institutes, literary clubs and corps of journalists had well-prepared the advanced sections of the working class to receive it.

Holyoake believed that the task of elaborating a Secular philosophy had now been completed for him. His duty was to simplify further and to propagate these doctrines. Eventually he was able to reduce the number of Secular principles to three: that the lives of men are improved by material means; that science, natural and social, is the source of the most reliable assistance to men; and that the greatest good is service to mankind. These propositions synthesized the Enlightenment, a benign view of human nature and English utilitarianism into an easily learned creed, philosophically unassuming, but a legitimate cousin of positivism's captivating formulas. Positivist societies and positivist churches were not founded in Britain until the 1860s; however, educated workingmen were increasingly adopting an ideology which can be labelled as positivist and which was best articulated by Secularism. It was not Holyoake, however, who was credited for expressing the ethos of the upper levels of the laboring class; this honor would be reserved for Samuel Smiles and his credo of self-help. In many respects similar to Secularism, self-help originated in Owenism and radicalism.[15] Associated as it was with atheism, Secularism could not have been applauded as was self-help by the Victorians.

That the working classes were indeed being lost to Christianity was no great surprise to mid-Victorian clergymen. For years they had observed that their pews were seldom warmed by the lower orders and that only infrequently were new churches built in urban communities. Yet it would be incorrect to underestimate the results of the religious census taken on Sunday, March 30, 1851. The report, consisting of over four-hundred pages of statistics and analysis, was not released until 1853. The one conclusion which was

so ominously clear was that nearly one-third of the population of
England and Wales had been inexcusably absent from church and
chapel on that Sunday. Although this document has been subjected
to much criticism by historians, its conclusions are generally
accepted as being substantially correct. [16] The majority of those
willfully absent from services had been of the laboring classes. Of
special interest to Holyoake was the reference made to his work.
Secularism, stated the report, "is the creed which perhaps with most
exactness indicates the faith which virtually though not professedly
is entertained by the skilled and unskilled laborer alike." [17] Holyoake denounced the report for inaccurately characterizing the
intellectual capacity of workingmen, but he did believe that its statements about Secularism were valid. [18]

Even without such publicity from the Crown, Secularism was
drawing the attention of increasing numbers of clergymen, especially
from those of the dissenting sects. During 1853 Holyoake was
challenged to several debates—offers which he gladly accepted
knowing that the publicity would assist him to popularize Secularism. Reverend Brewin Grant, a Congregationalist from Birmingham,
had already requested Holyoake to join in a public debate. After
wrangling during the autumn of 1852 about the issue on which they
would contend, the debates finally commenced. On six successive
Thursday evenings beginning on January 20, 1853, Holyoake and
Grant addressed themselves to the question, "What advantages
would accrue to mankind generally and the working class in
particular, by the removal of Christianity and the Substitution of
Secularism in its Place"? [19] Held at the Royal British Institute in
London, each session was attended by an estimated three thousand
auditors. Grant had painstakingly studied each past volume of the
Reasoner, and he now attempted to discredit Secularism by
revealing inconsistencies which he had discovered. Following traditional free thought practice, Holyoake sought to demonstrate that
Scripture was an offense to the rational mind, the old doctrines
superseded by scientific developments. Not only were the debates
reported by the evangelical newspapers—the *British Banner, Non-
conformist,* and the *Christian Times*—but also by the prestigious
Westminster Review which declared Holyoake the superior of the
two contestants. [20]

Reaction to Secularism by the clergy was not limited to debates.
On February 27, 1853, for example, London worshippers in
thirty-eight dissenting chapels heard sermons on the "Secular
Aspects of Christianity." [21] One of the most important responses

made to Secularism was that of the ecumenical Evangelical Alliance. Created in 1846 for the purpose of facilitating missionary activity, the Alliance now turned its attention to domestic infidelity. In 1853 a prize of £ 1,800 was awarded for the best monograph on the subject. Thomas Pearson, winner of the prize, concluded that infidelity was rooted in social discontent. Rather than a diatribe against freethinkers the book was really a denunciation of inactive, intolerant Christians for having prepared their society for Secularism.[22] Pearson's was not an isolated judgement. For example, Rev. H.A. Barnett, editor of the *Christian Advocate,* assured Holyoake privately that he and other Christians respected the Secularists even if they could not assent to their opinions.[23]

Other reactions were less pleasant. In its first number, the *London Quarterly Review,* an organ of the conservative Methodists, declared that "the author of the *Age of Reason* never uttered coarser and more offensive things regarding punitive dispensation of Providence than does the editor of the *Reasoner.*"[24] In November 1853 the *Reasoner* reprinted numerous articles concerning Secularism which had appeared in the *Unitarian Inquirer,* the *Aberdeen Herald,* the *Aberdeen Free Press,* the *Preston Guardian,* the *Coventry Herald* and the *Glasgow Examiner.* These commentaries usually claimed that the Secularist heresy could be explained by the failure of the church to adapt itself to rapid changes in British society.[25] Seldom was Holyoake condemned in such articles and he continued to do his utmost to avoid exciting hostile reactions.

His debates and consequent notoriety did bring Holyoake an enviable prestige among the Secularists. Wishing to reward Holyoake for having given them first-rate representation in the Grant debate, the London Secularists elected him president of their society and also presented Holyoake with the honor of a testimonial dinner on May 26, 1853. Thornton Hunt presided, Louis Blanc attended, and congratulatory messages were received from Robert Owen and Harriet Martineau. The epitome of the festivities was the awarding of £ 250 to Holyoake. This was not, however, a personal gift but was to be used only for "the furtherance of those principles we all have at heart." Responding warmly to such generosity, Holyoake commended their efforts, proclaiming that "the civilization of our time has isolated the working class and Secularism is the voice of their self-dependence."[26] The real task, he continued, was to propagate the liberating principles of Secularism among workingmen without, at the same time, establishing another sect to contend for their allegiance. Although he indicated that he had every intention of using this stipend to further the cause of Secularism, he would employ this money only as he saw fit.

The remainder of 1853 was highlighted by a debate at Newcastle in early August with Rev. J.H. Rutherford and by an extensive lecture tour in northern England and Scotland on which Holyoake was ably assisted by Robert LeBlond, a wealthy patron of the London Secularists.[27] Inspired by the enthusiasm of his predominantly working class audiences for Secularism and noting also that the circulation of the *Reasoner* had reached nearly five thousand per week, Holyoake resolved to establish a more systematic procedure for disseminating Secularism. With the £250 he had been awarded, Holyoake proposed to purchase James Watson's publishing concern. Watson, advancing in years, accepted the offer. In November 1853 Holyoake, with the assistance of his brother, Austin, founded the Secular News and Book Agency at 147 Fleet Street in London. Part of Fleet Street House—the name which Holyoake gave to his establishment—served as the print shop; other areas were utilized for a library, bookshop, and for assembly rooms for the London Secularists. Although he could have conceived of no more favorable a situation, Holyoake found that he needed more money. Necessary alterations of the property required an additional sum of £250 for which Holyoake did not hesitate to appeal to the Secularists.[28] He explained that the publishing business was not his for personal profit but that it was being conducted by him only to propagate Secularism. Legitimate liabilities, therefore, should be assumed by all Secularists. Not everyone agreed that Holyoake had acted wisely. He was highly respected, but many Secularists were not prepared to accept his dictum that the membership be expected to fund an operation over which they could exercise little direct control. Others believed that a publishing company was not a desirable activity no matter how efficiently it might be administered.

Holyoake might have found himself in an immediately defensive position, but, in the spring of 1854, he and other radical publishers enjoyed considerable prestige. For some time, British attention had been turned anxiously toward Eastern Europe. When the Crimean War finally did begin in March, the desire for news from the front was very great indeed and every London publisher wished to meet that demand. For several years, Holyoake had been a member of the Association for the Repeal of Taxes on Knowledge, a branch of the old People's Charter Union. Originally composed primarily of radical publishers like Hetherington and Watson who had fought the battle of the Unstamped in the 1830s, the Association sought the elimination of the remaining duties on advertising, on paper and the abolition of the required one penny stamp. These taxes increased the cost of publication so much, they still contended, that few workingmen could regularly afford to buy newspapers. In February 1851 the Association had been officially constituted with T. Milner-Gibson as president, Francis Place as treasurer, and Charles Dobson Collet, the historian of the movement, as its secretary. [29] The general committee of the Association included a rather prestigious number of radicals: Joseph Hume, Thornton Hunt, G.H. Lewes, John Bright, Richard Cobden and Holyoake. In response to a request from the Parliamentary radicals in March 1851 the Prime Minister, Lord John Russell, appointed a Parliamentary Committee to inquire into the Newspaper Stamp acts. Upon the committee's recommendation the duty on advertisements was immediately abolished. Until 1854, the Association had to be content with partial victory.

In order to meet the demand for news about the Crimean War, the Lord Mayor of London began to have an unstamped newsheet printed. The radicals declared that they could justifiably do likewise. During 1854 and 1855, Holyoake published two unstamped papers for the Association: the *War Fly Sheet* and the *War Chronicle*. If he had been held liable to the full penalty for his offenses, the fines would have exceeded £600,000. [30] But in March 1855 the compulsory stamp duties on newspapers were repealed—a consequence more of popular demand for inexpensive news about the exasperating events in the Crimea rather than of the defiance of the Association. [31] The radicals, of course, insisted on taking credit for securing greater liberty of the press and Holyoake shared in their acclaim. But the war had other results as well.

The role which the British assumed in the conflict was of great importance to Victorian radicals. So engrossed were they in the events transpiring on the continent that their own programs for social and parliamentary reform were temporarily ignored. Holyoake was certainly no exception, for he consistently devoted space in the *Reasoner* to foreign affairs. For example, C.D. Collet wrote a series of articles on the "Eastern question" in 1853 and 1854 calling upon the British government to pursue a more active role in curbing reactionism, especially Russian preponderance, in eastern Europe. [32] Interest in European politics had been stimulated since 1848 by the revolutionaries who, driven from their homelands, found safety in London. Many of them became friendly with Holyoake; Louis Blanc, Louis Kossuth, Alexandre Ledru-Rollin and others visited Fleet Street House. Semi-revolutionary societies, such as the Polish Central Democratic Committee, were allocated space in the *Reasoner* to further their appeals for financial aid.[33] Although the great majority of radicals contended that revolution was unnecessary in Britain, they believed it justifiable on the continent where despots held sway. Holyoake, therefore, urged his Secularist readers to assist those intent on returning to Europe by helping to finance their schemes. When the Crimean war finally ended in March 1856, Holyoake protested the continued subjugation of Italian, Polish, and Hungarian peoples by refusing to illuminate his Fleet Street office for the celebration.

The War had been popular with many radicals and its mishandling by the British government provoked the radicals to demand reform of the antiquated administrative and inefficient military structures. If the war had once diverted their energy from domestic reform, the radicals returned to the subject, their interst reactivated by the plight of the common soldiers who were suffering in filth and disease and who had been needlessly sacrificed because incompetent aristocrats bungled their battle orders. A malfunctioning government, the radicals reasoned, demanded reform as much as despotisms begged for revolution. Confident that such measures would soon be forthcoming, Holyoake responded patriotically to Ledru-Rollin's highly critical treatise, *The Decadence of England*, by asserting that the British would renew their institutions by finally eliminating the aristocracy from its privileged position. Then, he predicted, "we will comb the mane of the old forest king yet, and get the cotton off it, and feed him on Cossack beef and grease him with Russian tallow, till he gets sleek and strong, and natural and his claws grow and his voice comes again."[34] Not since 1848 had there been such enthusiasm for reform. J.A. Roebuck's motion for investigation by a select committee of the House of Commons was one result; equally important was the regeneration of enthusiasm for Parliamentary reform and for the extension of the franchise.[35] When John Bright renewed his attack on privilege in 1857 he would find that radicals in both the middle and working classes were very receptive to his appeals.

His continuing concern in such matters did not prove beneficial to Holyoake either as the leader of the Secularists or as a publisher. Perhaps he allocated even more time to these affairs than he should have done because Holyoake was soon proven to be a most incompetent business manager. His friend and advisor, LeBlond, warned him repeatedly to be more demanding of his employees, and to dismiss those who served poorly. "You have done," scolded LeBlond on one occasion, "those things as a tradesman you ought not to have done." [36]

Already in July 1854, Holyoake was begging the Secularists for more aid. "Fighting for freethought, dying for it, will not save it. I need," he pleaded, "that somebody subscribes for it." [37] In a letter which circulated to selected "friends of Secular Progress," Holyoake admitted the full extent of his financial plight; the lease and new fixtures for Fleet Street House had cost £230, and £100 had already been lost in the actual operation of the business. [38] The original £250 gift had quickly given way to a debt of £1,000. Freethinkers had always subsidized, in a meager way, of course, the activities of their spokesmen, but a debt of 1,000 verged on the outrageous. Among some old Socialists, Holyoake's appeals must have evoked memories of Owen's requests for contributions to build Harmony Hall.

In January 1855 Holyoake made his financial status public, explaining that he had in no way anticipated such great monetary losses. He assured his readers that he could conduct an efficient business and still serve the societies as a frequent lecturer because Austin, who had been managing Fleet Street House for nearly four months, was a most capable superintendent; it was due, he noted, to Austin's credit alone that the debt had been stabilized. Believing there was a need to convince the Secularists that they had absolutely no reason to suspect his honesty, Holyoake invited two of the most prominent members of the London Secular Society—John Maughan, the vice-president, and William Turley—to audit his accounts. Their report stated that the accounts were in good order and, like LeBlond, the auditors requested the Secularists to reduce the debts which Holyoake had injudiciously assumed. [39]

Holyoake's business in Fleet Street, his unrhetorical style of debating and writing, and especially his lack of interest in fostering Secularist organization were creating the impression that his leadership was inadequate. No national Secular conference had been called since the one in Manchester. Had not Holyoake indicated that general conferences were to be held annually? Already in July 1854 Holyoake had been confronted with these grievances by the local membership of the Stockport society. They also presented him with a letter from Robert Cooper requesting that a general conference be immediately called at which the delegates would attend to the election of a new central board.[40]   One week later, an "adjourned" committee resolved that a national conference be held as soon as possible. Holyoake was not explicitly opposed to a conference or to a more formal structuring of Secularism, but he warned again that progress was endangered by "self-made obstacles" and by "blatant verbiage." [41]   There is no record that a national or even a regional meeting of Secularists took place. Despite his debt and the murmurings of discontent with his policies, Holyoake's situation at the beginning of 1855 was quite secure. He had been able in late 1854 to visit many societies and he had also been re-elected president of the London Secular Society.

If Holyoake had wanted to insure his status, he might have easily done so by calling for a national conference or by vehemently denouncing the church. It soon became apparent, however, that Holyoake was seeking to turn the Secularists away from their preoccupation with religious criticism and in the direction of political involvement. Many times he had encouraged Secularists to seek practical activity. This belief, his association with the radical publishers, and his interest in the Crimean war were primarily responsible for Holyoake's declaration that "politics is the second half of Secularism." [42]   The *Reasoner,* he announced, would soon be combined with a radical paper, *The Northern Tribune,* which was currently being published in Newcastle by Joseph Cowen and edited by the former Chartist, G.J. Harney. Cowen and Harney wanted to abandon the *Northern Tribune* because its circulation had declined to less than 2,000 per week. Intending to start a local paper, Cowen offered the *Tribune,* at no cost, to Holyoake.[43]   Not only would the revised *Reasoner* be a journal of freethought, but it would also contain original and reprinted articles written by Mazzini, Francis Newman and other men currently engaged in politics. The announced task of the new *Reasoner* would be to prepare the workingmen to assume greater significance in public affairs.[44]
Francis Newman, who had been interested in Secularism for several years, granted permission for his "Political Fragments"—articles on Palmerston, Gladstone, and foreign policy—to be reprinted. A frequent correspondent of Holyoake's, Newman expressed the high regard which middle class radicals had for the *Reasoner's* editor. "I think," complimented Newman,

you so remarkably unite the two qualities—uncompromising hostility to false or unjust *systems*, and a tender and just allowance for the *men* who carry on those systems—that I rejoice in your becoming a political spokesman for English operatives, who are too often carried away by violent invective against *persons*—invective which always fails to effect reform. [45]

The new *Reasoner*, printed on poorer quality paper to reduce costs, was first issued in April 1855. In addition to Newman who did have valid credentials as a freethinker, the mystical Mazzini was the other illustrious contributor. Hardly could one expect the selections from Mazzini's *Faith and the Future* which appeared in the *Reasoner* to be well received by the majority of Secularists. "Believe and act," Mazzini wrote. "That which Christ has done, humanity can do. Believe and conquer." [46] Could the editor of the chief Victorian freethought periodical expect his readers to delight in such advice? Sympathize as he might with the cause of Italian unification, no freethinker would readily accept Mazzini's program for universal progress.

Shortly after the *Reasoner* experienced these alterations, representatives from Lancashire Secular societies met with London Secularists at Fleet Street House to discuss the possibilities of calling a general conference. At this meeting, a provisional committee was appointed to contact each society about "the necessity of an efficient organization of the Friends of Secular Inquiry throughout Great Britain." [47] Although the Lancashire people had strong organizational aspirations, and even though Robert Cooper was elected to this committee, no announcement of a general conference was issued. Even if Holyoake had agreed to holding a convention at this time, an unforeseen series of calamities would have hindered his participation.

William Chilton, only two years older than Holyoake, died suddenly on May 28, 1855. For more than a decade the two men had worked closely together. Chilton's death was only the beginning of tragedy; shortly Holyoake experienced a re-occurrence of that temporary blindness with which he had been afflicted some years before. [48] On July 8, his son Max, only eight years old, was accidently run down by a cab, and died ten days later. He was buried appropriately enough in Highgate cemetery to the strains of a secular hymn written by Harriet Martineau and sung by C.D. Collet. Holyoake's usual serenity was completely destroyed. With the financial assistance of a few friends, Holyoake secluded himself in northern France for several weeks. By the first week of September, however, he had returned to Britain and was lecturing in Middlesbro'-on-Tees and Newcastle.

While in Newcastle, Holyoake received news of yet another loss. Austin's twenty-seven year old wife, Lucy, a very active member of the London Secular Society, had died in childbirth on September 23. She also was given a simple Secularist funeral. Finally, on November 1, 1855, William Ashurst, Owen's old solicitor and Holyoake's very good friend, passed away. The deaths of two members of the family and two trusted associates, the burden of debt, and the criticism of his Secular policies made Holyoake's admission that he was "in no very enviable situation," a great understatement.[49] It was not his way, of course, to dwell on the sorrowful past. Freethinkers were not without emotions or doubts; yet their faith in reason and progress apparently allowed them to recover their healthy optimistic state, whatever the nature of bygone tragedy. At this time, however, Holyoake was not receiving positive encouragement but an ever increasing measure of criticism.

For one thing, the content of the *Reasoner* disturbed the many Secularists who believed that the elimination of "priestcraft" was still their primary goal. W.H. Johnson, a prominent Yorkshire Secularist, expressed this opinion to Holyoake: "I tell you honestly that throughout Yorkshire there is one feeling against so much Newmanism in the *Reasoner,* what is wanted is some of your lectures in oftener, and make it livelier. At present it is too dull."[50] Newman was a true skeptic, but his prose was arid. What Johnson really meant was that Holyoake should forcefully attack religion using the time-tested freethinking practice of ridicule.

Not confining his criticism to correspondence, Johnson also began to publish an ephemeral Secularist paper, the *Yorkshire Tribune.* The party, he claimed, was disorganized; they should assault Christianity directly by hiring Secularist missionaries and by holding out-of-doors assemblies. Holyoake was making a serious mistake by encouraging the working classes to take political matters into their own hands. If political reform was what Secularists were about, he concluded, should they not be trying harder to cultivate a relationship with influential members of Parliament. In response to Johnson and to Robert Cooper who had recently begun his own Secularist journal, the *Investigator,* Holyoake warned against over-zealousness and accused them of creating divisions within Secularism.[51]

It was evident by the end of 1855 that Secularism would not be able to contain the incompatible aspirations of its leaders. Since 1852 the number of Secularists had been steadily increasing, although it is impossible to state with any degree of accuracy how many Secularists there actually were or how many societies existed because they assumed various names and they never had federated in any way. Holyoake made no attempt to calculate the progress of Secularism in numerical terms, but he did assert that Victorian society was being significantly modified by the Secularists. Clergymen seemed less confident of their beliefs, less bigoted toward freethinkers and increasingly rationalistic. Even the dissenters, Holyoake wrote, were becoming more tolerant of skeptics.[52] For a fact, Victorian churches were becoming much more conscious of their inability to attract working class families. Although the church would never experience great success, many clergymen were willing to adopt unorthodox methods to penetrate into the laborer's life. Holyoake recognized that an honest spirit of concern for the poor was being demonstrated by some clergymen.[53] At Oxford, for example, Rev. Charles Marriott had begun a novel cooperative system which Holyoake found commendable. He also had earlier confessed that the work of J.M. Ludlow and Maurice was basically "secular."[54] Convinced that it would be a serious mistake to reiterate the old condemnations of Christianity, Holyoake encouraged Secularists to work with anyone, regardless of theological advocacy, who demonstrated a desire to improve the lot of Britain's lower orders.

He was, nevertheless, obliged to respond to his Secularist critics. In September 1856, Holyoake published *The History of the Fleet Street House,* a capsule summary and defense of his activites since 1840. Included in this tract were the financial accounts of the first twenty volumes of the *Reasoner,* the sad narration of the history of his business and a confession that the liabilities had now reached £ 1,690. He guaranteed that, once the debt was abolished, control of the business would be given to a board of directors. To those who demanded Secular organization, Holyoake rejoined that "it has been taken—they desired that some central organization should exist, and it has been created . . . Books, tracts, issue from Fleet Street House, and it serves as a meeting place for reformers and revolutionaries."[55] If they permitted it to fail, the Secularists could be accused of testifying to the inadequacy of their principles. Whatever warnings he might at this time issue, however, Holyoake would have had difficulty convincing dissatisfied Secularists that he was not living like a pensioner—engaging in his own private political activities at their expense.

The *Reasoner* itself bore witness against him because almost every edition reported one or the other of his political interests. For example, Holyoake had joined the Sunday League in its effort to open parks, museums and bandstands for the enjoyment of workingmen on their one day of leisure. In September 1856 at the request of Mazzini, Holyoake launched a subscription drive for Italian freedom. He was involved in trying to influence Parliament to allow an affirmation to be substituted in court for the oath. Although the Secularists were certainly not opposed to these activities, they believed that Holyoake was being distracted from more important tasks. Any additional non-Secular pursuits by Holyoake would very likely result in open conflict. Holyoake was fully apprised of this feeling and he must have realized that many rank and file Secularists did not consider him indispensable. Therefore, his activities after 1856 point clearly to the conclusion that Holyoake's concern for Secularism had been eclipsed by other interests.

*****

In March 1857 the Whigs were defeated on a motion against their Chinese policy, and Lord Palmerston took his case to the country. The general election which followed was contested primarily on questions of foreign policy and patriotism. It has, however, been correctly noted that considerable attention was given to domestic issues. Holyoake, for example, advised the Secularists to support Whig candidates but admonished them to raise the issue of franchise reform.[56] On March 23, a contingent of electors from Tower Hamlets, the most populous borough in the kingdom, put Holyoake's name forward as a candidate. With great enthusiasm, Holyoake delivered his first truly political speech. There were, he asserted, six objectives which he would seek: (1) residential suffrage; (2) property rights for married women; (3) a program of home colonization to replace poor relief; (4) abolition of church rates; (5) substitution of the affirmation for the oath; and (6) free Sunday recreation.[57] There was really nothing extraordinary about this platform which combined standard radical objectives and several Secularist points. Most significant was Holyoake's statement about the franchise because it was a compromise, designed to appeal to middle class and moderate working class radicals. On the basis of these goals, Holyoake always contended that he was the first man who aspired to sit in Parliament as a representative of labor. [58]

Holyoake's candidacy, however, was shortlived for, on March 26, he withdrew in favor of Acton Smee Ayrton, a liberal Whig. "Can I promote your interests, or avoid harming them in addressing the Electors, or at the Hustings?" Holyoake wrote to Ayrton. "My reason for writing is to keep in sight the interests of the Liberal cause." [59] Holyoake had apparently been requested by moderate radicals to withdraw because his candidacy was weakening the chances of Ayrton, a man uncommitted to Palmerston's domestic policies, from being returned. Moreover, the chance of Holyoake being elected, even though he was well known, was slim because his objectives were too radical for most electors. J.B. Langley, the radical editor of the *Morning and Evening Star* had requested Holyoake to withdraw. "I do not think that the time has come," consoled Langley, "for us to be able to do anything of consequence— and to fail is to show weakness." [60] It would be incorrect to place undue importance on Holyoake's brief candidacy, but the election did raise the issue of political reform. More important, many middle class radicals, such as John Bright, were defeated because they declared against Palmerston. Driven to search for an issue and a new base of power, the radicals soon found the opportunity as the radical-labor alliance, so unacceptable to the Chartists in 1852, began to be reconstituted.

Holyoake was given little opportunity to dwell in political reveries. The Manchester Secular Society had called a conference of neighboring societies for June 28 and it was believed that a demand for a national meeting would soon be forthcoming. Somewhat dismayed, Holyoake made it known that no sectional association or convention had the authority to take such initiative. If the Manchester faction did call a national meeting, they would usurp the power of the central or provisional committee and introduce into Secularism "that irregularity which destroyed the prestige of Chartism . . ." [61] The conference, attended by Austin Holyoake, did not order a national meeting but decided instead to strengthen the societies located in Lancashire and Cheshire. Although this was a victory for Holyoake, he could not delight in it because the London Secular Society, which had always been so firm in his support, was experiencing difficulty. On July 6, 1857, the Society of Materialists was created by a faction which contended that the Secularists lacked organization, that a set of principles around which a corps of committed freethinkers could consolidate had not been established and that it was foolish to open membership to those who held "the most absurd spiritual fancies."[62] Just how well this new society fared is unknown; its inception helped, however, to destroy confidence in Holyoake's leadership.

Dissatisfaction in the London society and in the Lancashire societies was intensified by a peculiar incident. Thomas Pooley, an eccentric Cornish well-digger, had been arrested in May 1857 for scrawling the words "Jesus Christ" on a clergyman's gate. Although his trial indicated that Pooley was not altogether possessed of his mental faculties, he was nevertheless convicted of blasphemy and sentenced to serve twenty-one months in prison. The Secularists, with Holyoake recalling his own experiences of 1842, protested in their journals. In September, Holyoake journeyed to Plymouth and Devonport to question Pooley's family, the clergyman whose gate had been defaced and the judge who had presided at the trial. He concluded that Pooley should have been acquitted because he was mentally incompetent. Surprisingly, after his thorough investigation, Holyoake did not condemn the law under which Pooley had been sentenced.[63] Several months later Pooley was pardoned—a testimony not to the power of the Secularists but to the compassion of the judge. Although this case was a most trivial matter, it was of great importance to the Secularists because it seemed to indicate that so little had been accomplished; men could still be punished or persecuted for their religious opinions.

Robert Cooper's *Investigator* expressed the opinion of many Secularists when it quoted James Robertson, secretary of the Manchester district, on the Pooley affair. Robertson said:

> We must put to shame this insolent habit of intolerance; we must rescue English law from complete barbarism . . . To do this work of today (a favorite phrase of Holyoake's and probably used by Robertson to lampoon Holyoake) we, the Freethinkers and Secularists of England, must establish some great central power—some wider and stronger organization than yet exists, which shall cover, as with a sacred shield, at any moment, and in any corner of England, whoever may be made the target of that wanton and ignorant and brutal bigotry, which exercises authority only to abuse it. We shall be feared only when we are formidable.[64]

The very last thing which Holyoake wanted was that Secularists should be feared. At one time, freethinkers had caused men to fear them. The result was persecution and the rejection of rationalism. To return to those ineffective tactics would be folly.

Holyoake conceded that district organizations, centered perhaps in London, Manchester, Birmingham, Newcastle and Glasgow, could assist the propagation of Secularism. He also announced that Fleet Street House might be considered as a College of Propaganda—an institution to accredit lecturers, publish Secular works and provide headquarters for a central board. Propaganda and missionaries were the only necessities of national Secular activity, and these would be supplied. Centralized organization was definitely to be avoided. "Organization," Holyoake warned, "ought not to degenerate into centralization. Local independent activity is the true thing wanted, and best adapted to Freethinkers." The function of Fleet Street House, he continued, "would be required, though no Secular Society existed anywhere, and it will be equally required when a hundred are in operation."[65] Holyoake would not be coerced into going further for two reasons. He did not believe that a centralized organization was the correct step to be taken and he also realized that he lacked the ability to direct the type of federation which Cooper and others were demanding.

Preoccupied with political affairs during the winter months of 1858 (see Chapter V), Holyoake was jolted back to Secular reality by a letter which Robert Cooper demanded that he publish in the *Reasoner*. Climaxing the attack of all those who had been dissenting from Holyoake's policies, Cooper furiously denounced him.

> You usurped, by a coup d'etat a Secular despotism, *no Freethinking Congress having appointed you to your position in Fleet Street.* You monopolized the funds—for a considerable time you monopolized its presses—you disparage its advocates . . . while pretending to be the embodiment of toleration, courtesy, and fair play, you are ever trying to smite down by innuendo every co-worker who refuses not merely to think after your measures but write after another style . . . after what has passed, however, I have no alternative but to withdraw my name from a movement which permits one of its representatives to use soft words to renegades (this is probably a reference to Thomas Cooper, the old freethinking Chartist, who was converted by the Baptists but who remained on very cordial terms with Holyoake)

> while he maligns those who have scorned to betray
> it and proved their sincerity by a life of service.[66]

His business failures, his lack of interest in organization and his vow to establish no criteria of membership left Holyoake defenseless in the face of these accusations. Shocked at the charge of despotism, Holyoake retorted that, as editor of the *Reasoner,* he always reserved the right to reject any communication which he deemed unfit for publication or which was not submitted in the spirit of honest controversy. Were the Secularists to be only a group of freethinkers and atheists devoting their efforts strictly to combatting the various forms of Christianity, or was Secularism to include all who acknowledged that human life and society were improvable and who demonstrated their willingness to work toward that end? Secularists, Holyoake was convinced, must decide if they were to become a club for atheists or if they were to welcome the cooperation of all who desired reform.

Holyoake had made his own position clear on many occasions. "To make Atheism the Shibboleth of the Secular party," he warned in March 1858, "would be to make Secularism an atheistic sectarianism as narrow and exclusive as any Christian Sectarianism. The principles of Secularism are distinct both from Atheism and Theism, and there can be no honest, useful, wide, and liberal party without keeping this point well understood."[67] Uncomplemented by an active concern for practical humanitarianism manifested in political or social action, Atheism was no more than blind iconoclasm. Those who refused to accept his judgment condemned "Secularism to the ranks of exclusive sectarianism; waiting for the descent of Aaron's rod, which shall swallow up all the rest. The scramble for this rod has kept the world in confusion 4,000 years."[68] The issue was now clearly drawn; Holyoake waited for the membership to render their decision.

In the divided London Secular Society a sizeable faction still supported Holyoake. To demonstrate their confidence, they succeeded in collecting £ 500 to guarantee that a "Central House for the Communication and Propagation of free opinion, to be conducted on unsectarian principles" would be continued.[69] They were, however, in the minority. At the semi-annual meeting on April 25, 1858, young Charles Bradlaugh, who had been lecturing and writing for several years under the pseudonym, "Iconoclast," was elected president of the London Secular Society. His first official act was to have the offices of the London Society removed from 147 Fleet

Street.[70] For several more years, Holyoake's name would continue to be associated with British Secularism in the public mind, but within the movement he occupied a secondary position.

*****

Bradlaugh, not yet twenty-five years old, had been born in London in 1833. As a boy, he had been oriented positively toward religion and had even been a Sunday School teacher. When, however, he questioned his minister about the validity of all Thirty-Nine Articles, Bradlaugh was suspended from his post, denounced to his parents and eventually driven from his home. In his quest for help, Bradlaugh sought out Richard Carlile, the same man who had befriended Holyoake at his trial in 1842. Through Carlile, Bradlaugh was exposed to free thought and by 1850 he was already lecturing in the London atheist assemblies.[71] His first performance—a lively discourse on Shelley—was delivered at a meeting on October 10, 1850, which was presided over by Holyoake. Soon Bradlaugh fell into debt and to escape his creditors, he enlisted in the Queen's service. After completing his military duties in 1853, Bradlaugh made his way back to London where he quickly attracted a following because he was an orator of the first rank. It was in freethinking circles that Bradlaugh developed the rhetorical skills which he later demonstrated in Parliament.

Like Holyoake, Bradlaugh was very interested in political affairs. During the early 1850s he was an advocate of the Sunday League's program; he also was acquainted with the continental revolutionaries and their schemes. Although they shared similar political concerns, the relationship between Bradlaugh and Holyoake was always uncertain. Bradlaugh was respectful of Holyoake and Holyoake confessed that Bradlaugh's abilities were unequalled, but they were men of very diverse temperaments. Inclined to vigorous denunciations of his opponents, Bradlaugh found Holyoake's style bland and compromising. Because Holyoake did indeed exercise a monopoly of the Secularist press, he presented a hindrance to Bradlaugh's advancement. In 1857 for example, Holyoake refused to publish Bradlaugh's *The Bible: What It Is: Being an Examination thereof from Genesis to Revelation,* because he feared that many readers would be offended by its vehement ridicule of Scripture.[72] Rebuffed by Holyoake on this and other occasions, Bradlaugh welcomed Robert Cooper's offer to write for the *Investigator.*

Bradlaugh's views on the character of Secularism were as clearly stated as Holyoake's. "There is," Bradlaugh claimed, "no middle ground between Atheism and Theism. The genuineness and authenticity of the Scriptures are questions relevant to Secularism. It is as necessary for the Secularists to destroy Bible influence as for the farmer to endeavor to eradicate the chickweed from his clover field."[73] Holyoake, of course, was committed to the position that theology was of minimal concern to the true Secularist. Although both men fought for the social and intellectual progress of the British working class and both engaged in practical politics, Bradlaugh contended that it was first necessary to free men from all religious encumbrances before progress could commence. Bradlaugh's victory over Holyoake in 1858 indicated that most Secularists agreed with him. Holyoake had allowed his attitude toward Christianity to evolve considerably in the past years, but he had not made a great enough effort to change the views of his disciples.

After Bradlaugh became president of the London Secular Society, Holyoake was still determined that Secularism should not become a society of atheists. In June 1858 one of Holyoake's most important but seldom read books, *The Trial of Theism* was published. The Christian and the atheist were equally obligated to make an affirmation about the existence of God. Secularism's great value, Holyoake insisted, was that useless controversy could be avoided by rejecting this question. One by one he reviewed and rejected each of the arguments presented by atheists and theists. Like other Victorian intellectuals, he confessed that "the existence of God is a problem to which the mathematics of human intelligence seems to furnish no solution. On the threshold of the theme we stagger under a weight of words."[74] The question was beyond the world of phenomena and, therefore, was meaningless to the positivist Holyoake. He was still compelled, however, to formulate an answer to that crucial Victorian problem of the origin of the Universe. "I am driven," he wrote

to the conclusion that the great aggregate of matter which we call Nature is eternal, because we are unable to conceive a state of things when nothing was . . . self extension is the most majestic of attributes and includes all others. That which has the power to exist independently of a God, had doubtless the power to act without the delegations of one. It therefore seems to me that nature and

God are one—in other words, that the God whom
we seek is the Nature which we know. [75]

Holyoake wished to avoid being pegged as an atheist or a pantheist.
His statements made it impossible for him completely to escape such
categorizations, but he avoided the issue when possible and wished
that all Secularists would do likewise.

At the end of May 1858 Holyoake's health once more
deteriorated. Suffering from nervous and physical exhaustion,
Holyoake left London with every intention of spending the summer
at the quiet village of Silloth. Austin was unable to provide his
brother with any good news from London.

> Now in consequence of your illness the only paid
> advocate of Freethought in the country is Brad-
> laugh and he does not so much. There is [sic]
> therefore very few societies left, and what are
> dragging out a miserable existence, are so few in
> number that they are scarcely observable. At
> Cleveland Street the average audiences number *30*,
> and they cannot get money to build the new Hall
> with. At Edgeware Road they are doing nothing. At
> Philpot Street they are on the point of closing.
> South London *is* closed and will be sold tomorrow
> or Monday. The business in the shop is propor-
> tionately depressed. What is taken from the Trade
> is two-thirds *less* than it was three years ago, and
> about one-half *less* than it was two years ago. And
> this is a true index of the state of the movement . . .
> The day of the half-religious, half-freethinking
> people appears to be coming. [76]

Percy Greg, an enthusiastic young Secularist who later became a
spiritualist, had been selected to edit the *Reasoner* in Holyoake's
absence. In addition to the other depressing news, Greg's performance was soon found to be most unsatisfactory; the sales of the
Reasoner continued to decline and Austin had to relate that
"business is very bad."[77] On August 14, Holyoake resumed his
editorial duties even though his health had not improved. Because
he interrupted his convalescence prematurely, Holyoake delayed his
full recovery for more than a year. He lectured infrequently and
seldom appeared in public. One of his few appearances was the
funeral of Robert Owen who died on November 17, 1858. Robert
Dale Owen, William Pare, Robert Cooper and Holyoake were the
official mourners at this solemn occasion.[78]

The Secularists scarcely noted Holyoake's return to London. Bradlaugh was exciting more enthusiasm than Austin had indicated. During Holyoake's period of diminished activity in 1858 and 1859, the *Reasoner* contained several glowing reports of Bradlaugh's orations. As an exuberant Oldham correspondent claimed, "we have never heard him surpassed." Without a doubt, Bradlaugh's popularity was rapidly advancing. At Doncaster, on September 28, 1859, eight thousand people listened to him condemn Christianity. On the same day, Holyoake spoke in York to an audience of less than one hundred on the progress made by the working class in his lifetime. [79]

Bradlaugh's reputation was also enhanced in 1859 by the invasion of revivalists. Holyoake ignored the evangelists, dismissing their zealous work as mere quackery in soul saving, but Bradlaugh responded. For example, on October 13 at Glasgow, four thousand applauded his tirade against the revivalists who were indeed effecting an extraordinary response in England. [80] Evangelical preachers were very successful in gathering large, eager audiences in open fields and in tents to hear their messages of salvation. Every Protestant denomination in England increased its membership; the new awakening also produced new techniques, such as those which would soon be carried out in London's East End slums by William Booth, to bring Christianity to every level of the urban population. Bradlaugh, utilizing many of the same flamboyant oratorical techniques as did the evangelists, was considered by the Secularists to be an ideal man to respond to this new challenge to rationalism.

Because his appearances were drawing great crowds in 1859, Bradlaugh was referred to by the Secularists as "our fearless and eloquent advocate." Comparing him to Holyoake, a Glasgow resident observed that "never in twelve years have lectures been so well attended . . . Mr. Bradlaugh is, I think, well cut out as a pioneer. Let Mr. Holyoake follow up as a builder, and we are likely to have a healthy movement with an organization amongst its members." [81] These communications must have been irksome to Holyoake, but had he not printed them in the *Reasoner* he would have been accused of trying to destroy Bradlaugh's popularity. His answer to Bradlaugh was contained in one further exposition of his beliefs, the *Principles of Secularism*. Secularism, Holyoake declared, had advanced beyond iconoclastic atheism by relegating all theological and metaphysical questions to history and by seeking to discover the laws regulating social behavior. In a few terse aphorisms, Holyoake developed his secular philosophy:

> Nature is.
> That which *is*, is the primary subject of study.
> The study of Nature reveals the laws of Nature.
> The laws of Nature furnish safe guidance to humanity.
> Safe guidance is to authority, not of names, but of Nature.
> For authority, Nature refers us to Experience and to Reason.
> For help, to Science, the nearest available help of man.
> Science implies disciplined powers on the part of the people, and concert in their use, to realize the security and sufficiency necessary to happiness.
> Happiness depends on moral, no less than on physical conditions.
> The moral condition is full and fearless discharge of Duty.
> Duty is devotion to the Right. Right is that which is morally expedient. That is morally expedient which is conducive to the happiness of the greatest number.
> The service of others is the practical form of duty; and endurance in the service of others the highest form of happiness. It is pleasure, peace, security and desert.[82]

Holyoake certainly did not lack ability to express his ideas with utmost clarity and brevity; he could convince men of his truths, but Bradlaugh excited them.

Capitalizing on his recently earned prestige, Bradlaugh formed the *National Reformer* Newspaper Company. The *Investigator,* which he had inherited from Cooper in 1858, was abandoned. In March 1860, with the help of Secularists in Sheffield, Bradford and Halifax, Bradlaugh created a periodical of "advanced Liberal opinion." Moreover, the *National Reformer* was to be the antagonist of "every known religious system, and especially to the various phases of Christianity taught and preached in Britain."[83] It appeared first on April 14, 1860 with an immediate and impressive circulation of eight thousand.

Bradlaugh also issued notice that a national Secular conference was to take place in early October 1860. Holyoake had committed his assistance to Bradlaugh at a preliminary conference in July, but he later excused himself complaining that the intended conference would not be entirely representative of Secularist opinion. [84] This rebuff initiated one of many quarrels between the two men; the year ended with Holyoake publicly condemning Bradlaugh's demaguery. [85]

During 1859 Holyoake had been able to eliminate his debts. A subscription begun already in 1858 reduced his liabilities to £900. In April 1860 slightly more than £400 remained to be cleared. The subscription committee, headed by J.G. Crawford and William Turley, continued hard at work with the result that by December all but £45 had been paid to Holyoake's creditors. Although the source of these generous contributions is not known, relatively few people were involved. No doubt, his illness of 1858-1859 was the chief inspiration to his benefactors. Following the example set by Bradlaugh, a *Reasoner* Company was organized, with one-thousand shares at ten shillings each offered for sale. Holyoake, of course, was retained as the *Reasoner*'s editor. For six months more the *Reasoner* lingered on, concerned primarily with reporting the feeble progress of Sir John Trelawny's Affirmation Bill to eliminate the oath required of men elected to the House of Commons. On June 30, 1861, the *Reasoner* ceased. In coming years the *Reasoner* was occasionally revived for short periods whenever Holyoake found some financial support, but the recognized organ of Secularism was now Bradlaugh's *National Reformer*. From time to time Holyoake contributed to Secularist literature and at times he even became involved in party strife. Secularism was still important to Holyoake, and he continued to allow his time to be occupied by Secular questions. Nevertheless, he considered Secularism to be a domain over which other men now ruled.

The evaluation of Holyoake's life between 1852 and the demise of the *Reasoner* in 1861 must give him considerable credit for the flourishing of Secularism. He did not seek organization but his lectures, tracts and the *Reasoner* generated enthusiasm which contributed to the foundation of numerous Secular societies during these years. It is impossible, of course, to state with any accuracy how many societies were created or how many members they enrolled because these groups remained unaffiliated. Joseph Mc-Cabe estimated that about thirty-five societies were founded between 1853 and 1857; in 1856, there were, he claimed, thirteen branches of the London Secular Society. [86] Years later, in 1880, when Bradlaugh's National Secular Society had reached peak strength, only sixty-one societies existed which altogether could claim only about six-thousand members.

Holyoake was concerned not with Secular membership rolls but with the degree to which Secular principles were being disseminated throughout British society. He believed that, according to his standards, there had been a general increase in rationalism from the pulpit to the factory. That Secularism was widely accepted by the lower orders is supported by an analysis which the *Westminster Review* presented in early 1862.[87] Despite attempts to evangelize them and regardless of the increasing number of city missions, the working class had fallen further away from Christianity than they had been at the time of the 1851 religious census. The *Westminster Review* declared that among skilled laborers there was almost no attachment to any denomination and no concern for theology. Only by reading widely in his literature could one begin to realize the extent of the workman's skepticism. The *Westminster Review* correctly claimed that the strength of Secularism could not be judged by the number of its periodicals, the extent of their circulation or by membership files because "Secularism, by its very nature tends to indifferentism." Yet, the *Westminster Review* asserted, in comment reminiscent of its note on Owenism of some twenty years earlier, that "Secularism is the religion, or the no-religion, of a large minority of thinking artisans." Rather than being an innovator of ideas, Holyoake had fashioned a label and a few principles which correctly described the intellectual consciousness of the emerging labor aristocracy. Engineers and mechanics cared as little for atheism as they did for Christianity, but they were much concerned with their material and social progress. By his emphasis on humanity and duty, Holyoake might have been near the brink of creating a secular religion. No priesthood, cults or rituals— Comte's ludicrous contribution to positivism—would he have ever stood for in Secularism. To the end of his life Holyoake continued to assume that men were rational, that the passions could be subordinated to the intellect. Bradlaugh, however, knew otherwise. His Secularism was indeed a perversion of the original form.

Because Secularism did resemble positivism, Holyoake has been credited with creating a climate within which positivism could become established. Although he had no use for positivist churches, Holyoake always expressed respect for Comte even after Comte had transformed positivism into a cult. "August Comte," Holyoake wrote shortly before the demise of the *Reasoner,* "has not lived in vain. Positivism is a real thing . . . Nature is real, Duty is clear, Right has to be upheld, and acts of service inculcated." [88]   Many who later became affiliated with formal positivism in Britain looked to Holyoake as one who had guided them in that direction. [89]

The most important of Holyoake's contributions during these years was his help to the laboring classes in gaining respectability. The labor aristocracy was becoming discernable during the 1850's and by emphasizing self-help, morality, and seriousness—Victorian *virtu*—Holyoake demonstrated that workingmen were very much an integral part of British society. Even before Bradlaugh's ascendency, and before the Secularist phase of his career had closed, Holyoake had become involved again in practical activity. As Francis Newman had encouraged him to do, Holyoake was becoming more of a political spokesman for British workingmen.

NOTES TO CHAPTER FOUR

1 J.B. Bury, "The Science of History," *The Varieties of History*, ed. Fritz Stern (Cleveland, Ohio: World Publishing Company, 1956), p. 223.

2 J.B. Bury, *A History of the Freedom of Thought* (London: Oxford University Press, 1952), p. 178.

3 Martin E. Marty, *The Modern Schism* (New York: Harper and Row, Publishers, 1969), p. 92.

4 See F.B. Smith, "The Atheist Mission," *Ideas and Institutions of Victorian Britain*, ed. Robert Robson (London: G. Bell and Sons, Ltd., 1967), 205-35.

5 By far the most detailed examination of British Secularism is E. Royle, "George Jacob Holyoake and the Secularist Movement in Britain, 1841-1861," Unpublished Dissertation, Cambridge University, 1968. See also his *Victorian Infidels; The Origins of the British Secularist Movement, 1791-1866* (Totowa; Rowman & Littlefield, 1974).

6 J.M. Robertson, *A History of Freethought in the Nineteenth Century* (London: Watts and Co., 1929), pp. 295-96. A similar error was made by Henry Sheldon. *Unbelief in the Nineteenth Century* (New York: Eaton and Mains, 1907), p. 207. Holyoake was not the "prime mover" behind organized Secularism.

7 John Eros, "The Rise of Organized Free Thought in Mid-Victorian England," *The Sociological Review*, n.s., II (July, 1954), 98-120 and David Tribe, *One Hundred Years of Free Thought* (London: Elek Books Ltd., 1967), p. 18. Although this monograph is devoted to describing the recent activities of the NSS, the early chapters discuss its origins. Tribe is particularly unsympathetic to Holyoake.

8 *Reasoner*, XIV, No. 3 (1853), 347.

9 Walter Simon, *European Positivism in the Nineteenth Century* (Ithaca, N.Y.: Cornell University Press, 1963), p. 213.

10 August Comte, *The Positive Philosophy*, trans. Harriet Martineau (London: John Chapman, 1853), pp. vii-viii.

11 *Ibid.*

12 *Reasoner*, XVI, No. 21 (1853), 321. Harriet Martineau, who was well acquainted with Secularism, maintained a polite correspondence with Holyoake for years. See R.K. Webb, *Harriet Martineau* (London: Heinemann, 1960).

13 Comte, *Positive Philosophy*, II, 511.

14 *Ibid.*, 512.

15 Asa Briggs, *Victorian People* (New York: Harper and Row, Publishers, 1963), pp. 116-39.

16 K.S. Inglis, "Patterns of Religious Worship in 1851," *Journal of Ecclesiastical History*, XI (April, 1960), 74-86. See also G. Kitson Clark, *The Making of Victorian England* (New York: Atheneum, 1967), p. 149.

17 Great Britain, Sessional Papers, Vol. LXXXIX (Reports), December 1853, "Religious Worship," p. 162.

18 *Reasoner*, XVI, No. 15 (1854), 251.

19 *Report of a Public Discussion Between Reverend Brewin Grant and George Jacob Holyoake* (London: Ward and Co., 1853).

20   *The Westminster Review*, n.s. IV (July-October, 1853), 246-48.

21   *Reasoner*, XVI, No. 11 (1853), 164.

22   Thomas Pearson, *Infidelity, its Aspects, Causes, and Agencies* (New York: Robert Carter and Bros., 1854). See especially pp. 605-20 for Pearson's remarks about the Grant-Holyoake debate.

23   H.A. Barnett to Holyoake (August 10, 1853), No. 584, C.U.

24   *London Quarterly Review*, I, No. 1 (1853), 146-49.

25   *Reasoner*, XV, No. 20 (1853), 320-26.

26   *Ibid.*, XIV, No. 23 (1853), 378-82.

27   J.H. Rutherford and Holyoake, *Christianity versus Secularism* (London: Ward and Co., 1854). Rev. Rutherford was well respected by workingmen; later, he became an active leader of the cooperative movement.

28   *Reasoner*, XV, No. 21 (1853), 338.

29   Charlet Dobson Collet, *History of the Taxes on Knowledge. Their Origin and Repeal . . . With An Introduction by George Jacob Holyoake* (London: T. Fisher Unwin, 1899), I, 137.

30   Holyoake, *Sixty Years*, I, 287. He calculated his fine upon the number of papers printed. It is most unlikely that, had the tax not been repealed soon after, he would have had such an enormous penalty imposed on him.

31   Olive Anderson, *A Liberal State at War* (New York: St. Martin's Press, 1967), p. 172.

32   *Reasoner*, XVI, No. 3 (1854), 39-41.

33   Polish Central Democratic Committee to Holyoake (March 24, 1854), No. 650, C.U.

34   *Reasoner*, XVIII, No. 8 (1855), 113-114.

35   Excellent analyses of the effect of the Crimean War on British radicalism and reform are contained in Briggs, *Victorian People*, pp. 32-86; Anderson, *A Liberal State at War*, pp. 129-162; and Gillespie, *Labor and Politics*, pp. 110-130.

36   *Reasoner*, XVIII, No. 5 (1855), 76. Together with his criticism, LeBlond pleaded with the Secularists to contribute to the cause of the Fleet Street House. LeBlond was well respected and Holyoake apparently believed that, by publishing his criticism, sympathy might be evoked for the financial condition of the Fleet Street business.

37   *Reasoner*, XVII, No. 1 (1854), 1-2.

38   This circular, dated only 1854, was probably distributed in the latter part of the year, No. 723, C.U.

39   *Reasoner*, XVIII, No. 6 (1855), 91.

40   *Ibid.*, XVII, No. 4 (1854), 51-53.

41   *Ibid.*, No. 10 (1854), 148-51.

42   *Ibid.*, XVIII, No. 8 (1855), 120.

43   Joseph Cowen to Holyoake (February 12, 1855), No. 736, C.U.

44   *Reasoner*, XVIII, No. 9 (1855), 138.

45   *Ibid.*, No. 10 (1855), 154.

46   *Ibid.*, XIX, No. 12 (1855), 93.

47   *Ibid.*, 94.

48   Francis Newman to Holyoake (July 18, 1855), No. 775, C.U. In this letter, Holyoake is questioned about his affliction which he has

apparently had for several months.

49 *Reasoner*, XIX, No. 36 (1855), 263.

50 W.H. Johnson to Holyoake (October 17, 1855), No. 801, C.U.

51 *Reasoner*, XIX, No. 34 (1855), 266; No. 35 (1855), 274; No. 36 (1855), 285; and No. 37 (1855), 293-94.

52 *Ibid.*, XX, No. 26 (1856), 201.

53 See K.S. Inglis, *Churches and the Working Classes in Victorian England* (Toronto: University of Toronto Press, 1963). This well documented monograph confirms the opinion that Victorian clergymen were very much concerned after 1850 with reaching the working class.

54 *Reasoner*, XVI, No. 24 (1854), 385-86.

55 Holyoake, *The History of Fleet Street House* (London: Holyoake and Company, 1856), pp. 19-20.

56 *Reasoner*, XXII, No. 13 (1857), 49. See also Gillespie, *Labor and Politics*, pp. 110-130 for a detailed analysis of working class influence on this election.

57 Holyoake's Electoral Address (March 23, 1857), No. 907, C.U.

58 Holyoake, *Sixty Years*, II, 349-54. For a reaction to Holyoake's claim, see G.D.H. Cole, *British Working Class Politics, 1832-1914* (London: The Labour Book Service, 1914), p. 38. Cole considers Holyoake's candidacy to have been in the Chartist tradition rather than the beginning of independent labor activity. Gillespie, *Labor and Politics*, p. 126, agrees with Holyoake and calls him "altogether one of the most able and constructive of working class leaders in the third quarter of the century."

59 Holyoake to A.S. Ayrton (March 25, 1857), No. 908, C.U.

60 J.B. Langley to Holyoake (March 22, 1857), No. 902, C.U.

61 *Reasoner*, XXII, No. 26 (1857), 101.

62 *Ibid.*, No. 30 (1857), 135.

63 *Ibid.*, No. 39 (1857), 201-06.

64 Reprinted in the *Reasoner*, XXII, No. 41 (1857), 217-18.

65 *Reasoner*, XXII, No. 38 (1857), 193.

66 *Ibid.*, XXIII, No. 13 (1858), 103. An incident had occurred several years before which, while not directly relevant to Secularism, helps to clarify the reasons for the animosity between Holyoake and Cooper. Samuel Fletcher, an old Owenite, had followed the development of Secularism with great interest. In 1852, he made Holyoake the beneficiary of the magnificent sum of £30,000. In early 1856, Fletcher changed his mind and made Robert Cooper his beneficiary. In May, 1856, Fletcher died and, although I have no evidence, Cooper presumably inherited the money. Holyoake suspicioned that Cooper may have behaved in a manner unbecoming to a gentleman in persuading Fletcher to favor him but made no direct accusation to that effect because of the possibility that their rivalry would be solely attributed to this one incident and not to a matter of conviction.

67 *Ibid.*, XXIII, No. 11 (1858), 81-82.

68 *Ibid.*, No. 14 (1858), 105-06.

69 *Ibid.*, No. 17 (1858), 129. One donor, W.J. Birch, perhaps contributed £350.

70 *Ibid.*, No. 18 (1858), 143.

71 For the details of Bradlaugh's life, see Hypatia Bradlaugh Bonner and J.M. Robertson, *Charles Bradlaugh* (London: T. Fisher Unwin, 1895). This is a very sympathetic but nonetheless accurate account. Walter Arnstein, *The Bradlaugh Case* (Oxford: The Clarendon Press, 1965) deals almost exclusively with Bradlaugh's parliamentary career. It is unlikely that the definitive biography of Bradlaugh will ever be written because he destroyed most of his private papers before he died.

72 Bonner, *Bradlaugh*, I, 64.

73 *Ibid.*, 80.

74 Holyoake, *The Trial of Theism* (London: Holyoake and Company, 1858), p. 156.

75 *Ibid.*, p. 157.

76 Austin Holyoake to G.J. Holyoake (July 15, 1859), No. 1113, C.U.

77 Austin Holyoake to G.J. Holyoake (July 20, 1859), No. 1114, C.U.

78 *Reasoner*, XXIII, No. 48 (1858), 383.

79 *Ibid.*, XXIV, No. 42 (1859), 333; No. 41 (1859), 326.

80 *Ibid.*, No. 44 (1859), 349. An extensive account of the revivalists and of the response which they evoked is found in J. Edwin Orr, *The Second Evangelical Awakening in Britain* (London: Marshall, Morgan and Scott, Ltd., 1949).

81 *Reasoner*, XXIV, No. 47 (1859), 375 and No. 44 (1859), 346.

82 Holyoake, *Principles of Secularism* (Holyoake and Company, 1859), p. 40.

83 Bonner, *Charles Bradlaugh*, I, 120.

84 *Reasoner*, XXV, No. 33 (1860), 261.

85 *Ibid.*, No. 52 (1860), 414.

86 McCabe, *Life and Letters of Holyoake*, I, 297. These statistics are confirmed by Royle, "G.J. Holyoake and the Secularist Movement."

87 "The Religious Heresies of the Working Class," *Westminster Review*, n.s. XXI (January and April, 1862), 60-97.

88 *Reasoner*, XXVI, No. 1 (1861), 2-3.

89 Royden Harrison, *Before the Socialists* (London: Routledge and Kegan Paul, 1965), p. 319.

CHAPTER V

THE MAKING OF A WORKING-CLASS LIBERAL, 1858-1868

If there was a single issue which dominated domestic politics from the late 1850s until the mid-1860s, it was the extension of the franchise. Would a bill soon be passed? If so, how many new voters would be created and what effects would an expanded electorate have on the British constitution and political process? Never had the urban working classes given up their quest of the vote. Although numerous franchise bills were drafted between 1852 and 1866, the gentry-dominated Parliament regularly rejected them. Beginning in 1858, and especially after the *Reasoner* collapsed in 1861, George Jacob Holyoake devoted much of his attention to the franchise question. Although it cannot be claimed that he played a major role in the events which led to the Second Reform Bill, Holyoake did publish several widely considered essays on the subject; he was a ranking member of the Reform League; and, on one occasion, his actions did affect the course of events preceding passage of the bill. But more important, Holyoake provides the historian with an example of a significant and new element of the Victorian political spectrum—the working class Liberal. [1]

Only recently has the Reform Bill of 1867 attracted the interest of historians of nineteenth century British political development. Their centennial research has admirably filled what had been something of a historical vacuum. [2] These scholars agree that a combination of public restlessness and political maneuvering within Parliament were important factors in the passage of Disraeli's bill which doubled the size of the electorate, but their narratives differ in the relative importance which they assign to working class agitation and to professional politicking. Furthermore, these scholars have yet to arrive at a concensus about the motives of key individuals and parties both within and outside the House of Commons.

Holyoake's political activities, especially between 1861 and 1868, must be clearly delineated within the context of the struggle for franchise reform.[3] Professors Asa Briggs and F.B. Smith contend that the reform act is best understood as an adjustment of the political superstructure to fundamental social change. And Holyoake did articulate many of the attitudes toward franchise reform of that sector of British society which was to be taken within the pale of the constitution, namely, the labor aristocracy. By the end of the 1850s British artisans and mechanics—those sectors of the working class with whom Secularism is most clearly identified—no longer referred to themselves as ordinary laborers. Holyoake certainly can not be considered as a workingman; by any socio-economic standards he was a petty bourgeois, although he continued to claim status as a workingman. Without the emergence of the "better sort of working folk," perhaps no extension of the suffrage could have been peacefully obtained. Patronizing members of Parliament had come to believe, in the decade preceding 1867, that these men had proven themselves worthy of the franchise. The real problem for drafters of bills was to find a satisfactory formula which would limit any extension of the franchise to the labor aristocracy which in 1867 numbered approximately one-sixth of the British adult male population of 5,300,000.[4]

The labor aristocracy had not completely forsaken their Chartist heritage. Their goal was still universal suffrage, but they were by no means as defiant and as conscious that they belonged to a separate class as their Chartist forebears had been. The labor aristocracy was generally composed of reasonable men who believed in the British political tradition and who respected the law. Many, moreover, were also willing to accept a bill which granted something less than universal suffrage. The possibility should not be obscured, however, that this moderate attitude might be transformed into bitter hostility by an intransigent Parliament. The persistence of radical temperateness, even though Parliament did not respond to their appeals for the vote, must be attributed to the intentions of the leading agitators to restrain the more anxious of their comrades. Although the possibility of disorder existed in the years before 1867, only a few instances of it are recorded. Holyoake's counsel for moderation exemplifies that of most working class leaders.

His heightened interest in politics had several sources. First, there was the brief Parliamentary campaign in 1857. But it was actually in the following year that Holyoake became more actively concerned with franchise reform. During the winter of 1858, London radicals were anxiously awaiting the outcome of the trial of Felice Orsini who had attempted to assassinate Louis Napoleon in December 1857. The technically-minded Holyoake knew of Orsini's plan because he had been given the task by Orsini's co-conspirators of testing hand bombs, the very type which were used in the vain attempt. Holyoake was, however, much less aware of the details of the plot than were other British conspirators who had assisted Orsini.[5] Holyoake was never implicated by any testimony at the Orsini trial but it was very obvious that the plot had been prepared in Great Britain and that British citizens had been privy to its details.

In February 1858 Palmerston brought forward his famous conspiracy bill which provided harsh penalties for anyone conspiring to overthrow a legitimate foreign government. The radicals rose in protest against the bill not because of its terms but because it seemed so much like a personal favor to the despised emperor. On February 16, a meeting was held at Fleet Street House to plan a public protest for February 21 in Hyde Park; Holyoake took charge of printing the placards announcing the mass gathering. The threat of massive protest combined with a change in Parliamentary opinion brought about the defeat of Palmerston's bill and the government immediately resigned. Instead of a protest an orderly victory demonstration took place. Impressed with their success, the radicals, led by Ernest Jones, met on February 26 and formed the Political Reform League, an association to build public pressure for domestic reform. Holyoake was one of the charter members.[6]

Several months later, John Bright, who had been defeated at Manchester in Palmerston's triumph of March 1857, sought and easily won a vacant seat in Birmingham. Although he had been politically inactive for several years because of illness, Bright now was campaigning with a vengeance for reform. During 1858 he captivated his electors with his denunciations of artistocratic government and his ringing calls for a wide extension of the franchise. Since 1852, when the National Parliamentary and Financial Reform Union met its end, moderate working class radicals and middle class radicals had sought to cooperate. In the person of Bright, their quest was symbolically ended. Once the hero of Manchester, Bright was now the favorite of Birmingham. "The times," G.M. Trevelyan has explained, "were ripe for a union of the Radical part of the middle class with the workingmen; Bright was born and bred to preside over such a junction of forces."[7]

Bright, however, was no true democrat and when he finally did produce a franchise bill in January 1859, it called only for household suffrage. Many working class radicals believed that Bright, for all his boldness, was now retreating from his earlier promises to ask for nothing less than manhood suffrage. From this time on Bright's intentions were reviewed with some suspicion, but working class interest in reform had been rekindled. Although Holyoake was deeply enmeshed in Secularist affairs in 1858, he did produce the first of his important political tracts, *The Workman and the Suffrage.* There was little need, he wrote, for the upper classes to fear universal suffrage in a land where "so many people are uninformed, prejudiced, and indifferent upon politics that ignorance, animus, and bigotry may be relied upon to vote for things as they are." Holyoake certainly did not hold such a low opinion of British workingmen, but he did believe that they possessed a degree of reverence for law, rank and wealth unknown in other lands. If granted the vote, they would in no way use it to overturn the social system. He then went on to caution the working classes against obtaining the suffrage by force. A serious situation could result if the upper classes would be frightened into creating "new elements of corruption and intrigue in the state to circumscribe the operation of the dreaded franchise."[8] What these "new elements" might be Holyoake could leave to the imagination of his readers; before the secret ballot and legislative restrictions on corrupt electioneering, almost any form of voter intimidation or manipulation was conceivable.

By far the most important feature of *The Workman and the Suffrage* was Holyoake's scheme for enfranchisement. It made little difference, he claimed, if a reform bill were "based on a rating suffrage or rental" as long as it provided for "admission of all who may possess or acquire a certain intelligence qualification."[9] Holyoake proposed that the prospective voter be required to demonstrate his ability to explain a section of a well-known work on law or economics. To show that he understood a selection from Mill's *Political Economy,* for example, would not have been inordinately difficult for many a self-educated workingman but for the ordinary laborer an incredibly awesome task. This provision also was thought to have the advantage of not frightening the upper classes because the electorate would continue to be composed of the literate and well-educated. The ignorant who might be expected to vote foolishly would be denied the privilege. Reflected by *The Workman and the*

Suffrage was the self-help ethic of the labor aristocracy to whom a self-acquired right of voting had an obvious appeal; it was another mark of independence. Samuel Smiles' notions which he presented in *Self-Help* (1859), the most popular of numerous examples of self-help literature, appealed to a goodly number of workingmen as well as to the Victorian bourgeoisie.[10] It must be remembered, of course, that laboring men, in spite of adopting this and other predominantly middle-class values, retained their traditions of collective action. For Holyoake to have asserted that a man be required to demonstrate literacy and his comprehension of basic economic and political concepts before being admitted to the electorate was just as logical as the stipulation that an elector have attained a certain level of wealth. Any bill embodying this proposal would also tend, Holyoake believed, to lessen the worship of property; men would be encouraged to develop their minds. He was not disturbed that suffrage would not immediately become universal. In time, as the percentage of the educated increased, only those would be denied the vote who gloried in their ignorance.

Although Holyoake's treatise did not advocate universal male suffrage, it did appeal to a good many working class readers because of its emphasis on self-help. But neither was it unpopular with the Tories who in 1859 presented their own enfranchisement bill. In his defense of the bill's complicated and moderate provisions, Disraeli spoke disparagingly of democracy:

> I have no apprehension myself that if you had manhood suffrage tomorrow the honest, brave, and good natured people of England would resort to pillage, incendiarism and massacre. Who expects that? ... Yet I have no doubt that ... our countrymen are subject to the same political laws that affect the condition of all other communities and nations. If you establish a democracy you must in due course reap the fruits of a democracy.[11]

Lord Stanley, Derby's son, who assisted Disraeli in drafting the bill of 1859 took the liberty of quoting from *The Workman and the Suffrage* during debate in order to demonstrate that even a man of "extreme political opinions" was in agreement with a gradually expanding franchise. After referring to John Stuart Mill's elitist scheme for granting multiple votes to the educated, Stanley noted that Holyoake had insisted upon "'an expansive suffrage which shall be open to the worthy and shut out the unfit.'"[12] The 1859 bill, however, really pleased no one and Lord John Russell's motion against it succeeded in bringing down the Derby government.

In March 1860 Russell put forward his own bill based upon a £6 rental qualification for the boroughs and a £10 for voters in the counties. It likewise received little support and was soon withdrawn. For the duration of Palmerston's ministry, there was no chance for a franchise bill to succeed. Palmerston's ministry, symbolizing British supremacy as it did, was strong and popular. Even the radicals seemed to be under the spell of Palmerston. As long as he was the Prime Minister, it was unlikely that any reform bill would succeed. Commenting on the necessity of reform in 1864 Palmerston remarked, "Oh there is really nothing to be done . . . We cannot go on adding to the Statute Books *ad infinitum.* Perhaps we may have a little law reform, or bankruptcy reform; but we cannot go on legislating forever." [13] When the Parliamentary radicals raised no complaint after Russell's bill was withdrawn, complacency solidified under the last years of Palmerston's leadership; no further attempt to extend the franchise was made until 1866.

Holyoake, like many radicals, turned to other affairs. Between 1859 and 1861, it must be remembered, he was ill and was also involved in the winding up of the *Reasoner.* He continued to be occupied with Secularism for a time. In late 1861, Bradlaugh, in an attempt to consolidate the Secularist party, convinced Holyoake to become a chief contributor to the *National Reformer.* In January 1862 Holyoake's views of the nature and purpose of Secularism began to be a regular feature of the journal. This cooperative venture was terminated in April, however, because Bradlaugh insisted that Holyoake refer to the *National Reformer* as the "advocate of Atheism." [14] Miffed, Holyoake resigned but demanded that £2 per week, for which he had contracted with Bradlaugh, be paid during the remainder of the year. When Bradlaugh refused, Holyoake called in a lawyer and eventually Bradlaugh was persuaded to pay him £81. Such petty squabbling could hardly be expected to have a positive effect on the Secularist rank and file.

After this episode—and for the next two years—Holyoake wrote for a variety of newspapers. He reported prizefights, public hangings and royal marriages. The most important publication for which he wrote was the moderately radical *Newcastle Daily Chronicle and Northern Advertiser* published by Joseph Cowen, Jr. In addition to free-lancing, Holyoake produced over two dozen pamphlets between 1861 and 1864 on free thought, cooperation and the affirmation bill which Sir John Trelawny was attempting to pilot through the House of Commons.[15] Although franchise reform was a temporarily forgotten issue, two developments took place between 1859 and 1864 which proved to be of utmost importance. First, the development of the "new model" unions, especially after the London builders strike of 1859-1860, contributed to the politicization of the working class. The Amalgamated Society of Carpenters and Joiners, led by Robert Applegarth, and the Amalgamated Society of Engineers sought to organize the labor market and to institute collective bargaining procedures. Applegarth, who boasted that his union consisted "of the superior class of workmen," also insisted that laboring men become first class citizens; therefore, they must have the franchise.[16] The campaign for Italian unification and the American Civil War also stimulated working class interest in domestic reform. Both the war in the U.S. and the Italian struggle were represented as conflicts between democracy and privileged orders. British workingmen were prompted to reflect more seriously on their own political status.

The working classes had been very interested in European affairs since 1848 and they were especially attracted by the course of Italian events, even rendering enthusiastic but unimportant assistance to Garibaldi in his campaign for Italian freedom and unification. Holyoake was secretary of a committee which recruited a volunteer legion in September 1860 to go to Italy and serve under Garibaldi.[17] A thousand British "excursionists," poorly equipped and inadequately officered, actually did participate in one minor skirmish against the crumbling Bourbon army. Excessively romanticizing their contribution to Italian liberty, British workingmen were naturally wild with enthusiasm when they learned that Garibaldi intended to visit England in April 1864. In a score of cities, committees prepared great demonstrations to honor Garibaldi; upon his arrival in London, an escort of twenty-thousand workingmen greeted him.[18]

Fearing that such fervor for revolutionaries and for democracy might be easily misused by unscrupulous demagogues, the apprehensive Whig ministry requested Garibaldi to terminate his visit at once. The remainder of his itinerary was cancelled. Laboring men everywhere, especially those who had planned elaborate festivities, were indignant that they should have been deprived of honoring the heroic Garibaldi. To protest the government's decision a demonstration was scheduled to be held at Primrose Hill on April 23, 1864. Presiding over the gathering was Edmond Beales (1803-

1881), a man long active in promoting support for revolutionary movements in Poland and Italy. The crowd, however, was immediately dispersed by the police on the grounds that it was illegal to hold discussion of "popular and exciting topics" in the public parks.[19] Enraged by this affront, Beales and the committee which had organized the Primrose Hill meeting continued to meet regularly during the remainder of 1864. The topics of franchise reform and the secret ballot were soon added to their agenda. In February 1865 these radicals including ex-Chartists, members of the Political Reform League and the well-organized trade unionists founded the National Reform League. Bradlaugh and Holyoake were both selected to serve on the League's governing council. Never had the working class radicals been so unified or blessed with such competent leadership.

At this time, Holyoake produced his second political pamphlet, *The Liberal Situation: Necessity for a Qualified Franchise.* Beginning by condemning workingmen for their past years of apathy regarding the franchise and continuing by denouncing the government for denying the franchise to laboring men, this document reflected the moderate but persistent mood of the new National Reform League. John Stuart Mill, who had recently made several financial contributions to Holyoake's publishing activities, informed Holyoake in late April 1865 that he considered *The Liberal Situation* to be "one of the best of your writings and well calculated to stir up the thinking minds among the working classes to larger views of political questions."[20] Holyoake again suggested that an examination device could best reduce the problems facing the Whig-Liberal party. Manhood suffrage would give the working class immediate numerical superiority in most constituencies but a precipitous change in the composition of the electorate would be mitigated by the use of a test.[21] To those who could accept nothing less than universal manhood suffrage, Holyoake's position seemed to be sabotaging the effectiveness of the League. Although he did desire universal suffrage—Holyoake would have demanded that women too be enfranchised—the chances for such a victory were very remote. Inevitably, there would be limitations. How much better it would be, therefore, to make those restrictions of a non-materialistic nature.

The "advanced Liberals" in the House had allowed the reform question to lie idle for several years but, in the spring of 1865, Sir Edward Baines moved his Borough Extension Bill which would have reduced the £10 rating qualification for the franchise to £6. The enemies of reform, especially the dissident Whigs, were against such wholesale enfranchisement and used Holyoake's *The Liberal Situation*, taking its passages completely out of context, in their arguments. On May 3, 1865, Robert Lowe, the future leader of the "Adullamites" and an extreme reactionary, referred to a statement in *The Liberal Situation* in which Holyoake had condemned Frenchmen who had used the franchise to vote away their own liberty.[22] Several days later on May 8, W.H. Gregory, another dissident Liberal, quoted lengthy sections of Holyoake's tract. Holyoake, he claimed, was a man of "extremely liberal" opinion and "who wrote with great vigor" on behalf of working class causes, but who opposed extending the franchise by lowering property qualifications.

> 'No partial enfranchisement can produce direct political improvement when large enough to effect a substantial transfer of power . . . There may be no reason to refuse partial enfranchisement; but it would be as indecent in the working classes to exult in it as it would be in ten men who were taken from a wreck by a choice of the captain, and who should throw up their caps in the face of all those left to their fate.' These were the words of Mr. Holyoake. [23]

Of course Holyoake was not in favor of partial enfranchisement although he did believe it was the only immediately realizable goal. He did oppose partial enfranchisement if it were achieved only by reducing property qualifications.

Gregory then continued by quoting Holyoake's own estimate in *The Liberal Situation* of radical attitudes toward a wholesale extension of the franchise.

> 'I know towns where ardent Reformers are themselves afraid of an unqualified franchise. Good Radicals, the most thorough of their class, have said to me, "There is a mob in our town (there is in every town), ignorant, selfish, venal, and reckless of principle; had they all votes, our present Liberal Members would be unseated at the next election. They would vote against those who seek to raise them". This is a general feeling in Liberal boroughs. Now there is no plan of a £6 suffrage which selects the worthy and excludes the base. All £6 suffrage is blind; and hence we have Radicals

> arguing feebly and fearing much the result of the
> very measure they plead for. Surely this is political
> imbecility. This is the real dilemma which ought to
> be put an end to by adopting a plan of protective
> suffrage, of which the only opponents are Radicals
> whose policy has long undergone petrification.' [24]

Gregory's strategy was obviously to discredit the Liberal measure by
presenting their own qualms about the bill. Holyoake's stand,
expressed in *The Liberal Situation*, was perhaps unfortunate but
understandable because he was trying to develop the rationale for an
educational test which he believed so much more preferable to
property qualification. Certainly some advanced Liberals did fear
immediate democratization. They well knew how voters could be
bought and influenced, but it was incorrect to portray Holyoake and
other Liberals as opponents of democracy. In any case, Baines'
motion was easily defeated on its second reading, but the issue of
franchise reform was nevertheless very much alive again.

Although the Reform League was officially committed to
universal suffrage, Beales and quite probably a majority of its
council recognized that partial enfranchisement was the only
possibility. By and large they agreed with the admonition once given
to them by John Bright:

> I think you are quite right to move for manhood
> suffrage for that is what you must approve . . . I
> think the people everywhere should ask for what
> they want, but at the same time, I would recom-
> mend that they who ask for much should not
> regard as enemies and opponents those who ask for
> less. By a combined and friendly movement we
> shall get something, and that once gained is never
> again lost, but becomes an additional power to
> obtain more. [25]

Similar advice had of course been given by Holyoake to the Chartists
who were being courted by the National Parliamentary and Financial
Reform Association in 1852. In 1865 the Reform League, composed
primarily of working class radicals faced a serious tactical question.
Would the moderates—the labor aristocracy—be able to retain
control of the League and, at the same time, agitate effectively for
franchise reform? This question was of the greatest importance in
1865 and 1866. Agitation was certain, and it could lead to violence.
But if the demonstrations by the League were too passive, their
demands might again be ignored. As Professor Cowling has

reminded us, Parliament did not fear agitation, but agitation was a component of public opinion with which Parliament interacted.[26] The long denied franchise, rising levels of unemployment due partly to the American Civil War, and immoderate statements made by M.P.'s who opposed reform could operate together to provoke a reaction from the militant members of the League. The relationship between the Reform League and Parliament was crucial for, although agitation was necessary, a display of violence might lose for the working classes their greatest asset: the image of respectability.

The middle class and parliamentary radicals were drawn closer to the League by the general election of July 1865. Holyoake's assistance was requested by several candidates. P.A. Taylor, a radical from Leicester, received Holyoake's help on his campaign address. Thomas Hughes, prominent Christian Socialist and author of *Tom Brown's School Days*, requested Holyoake to assist in his campaign among the Lambeth electors. "I am writing in some anxiety for news from you," communicated Hughes, "when shall I go on the stump? or shall I meet any persons whom and where?"[27] Holyoake responded. A few days before the election, he went to Newcastle to campaign there on behalf of the Reform League for Joseph Cowen, Sr. Holyoake was a close friend of the younger Cowen and the elder had promised to consider Holyoake for the position of his Parliamentary secretary. Cowen, aged sixty-seven, won his contest and, against considerable criticism from the Newcastle press for appointing a notorious freethinker to such a post, he did fulfill his bargain with Holyoake in February 1866. The nature of Holyoake's duties and the exact length of service to Cowen is undetermined but Holyoake did use this opportunity to become acquainted with many members of Parliament, Conservative and Liberal alike.

Granted his final victory, Palmerston died on October 18, 1865. His passing signalled the beginning of another attempt to reform the franchise. The new Prime Minister, Earl Russell (formerly Lord John Russell), and W.E. Gladstone had been drawing closer to the working classes. In 1862 Gladstone had received a tumultuous welcome by Newcastle laborers, due partly to Holyoake's articles in Cowen's *Newcastle Daily Chronicle.* "I have no doubt," Cowen wrote to Holyoake, "what was done for him while here will urge him on in a radical direction."[28] By 1864 Gladstone had become a champion of electoral reform, startling the country by proclaiming, "I venture to say that every man who is not presumably incapacitated by some consideration of personal unfitness or political danger, is morally entitled to come within the pale of the constitution."[29] Gladstone's position on the American Civil War and his interest in European freedom had also contributed to his prestige among the working class radicals. With Palmerstone gone, Gladstone was now free to finish the creation of the Liberal party and to bring the long awaited reform bill to Parliament.

Like his predecessors, Gladstone hoped to construct a bill which, while admitting a substantial portion of the working class to the electorate, would not seriously alarm those already enfranchised.[30] The cabinet, as expected, was divided over the terms of the legislation and, because of the quantity of data accompanying it, the bill was delayed nearly six months. Finally, on March 12, 1866, a most moderate bill was presented to Parliament. Gladstone proposed that borough residents paying £7 in rent and householders in the counties paying £14 be enfranchised. If passed, the bill would have given the vote to one man in four instead of one in five. Thus, a modest, but not insignificant, expansion of the suffrage was being requested.

The Reform League had been meeting frequently beginning in February 1866 to formulate the position which they would take on the expected bill. Holyoake, of course, took part in the deliberations.[31] Meanwhile, the radical, James Clay, had come forward with a bill of his own. While maintaining the existing £10 rental qualification, Clay's bill would have conferred the vote on any man who could pass an examination consisting of "writing from dictation . . .simple addition, multiplication, and division of money."[32] The proposed test was, in reality, more difficult than some Civil Service examinations. Holyoake, of course, was very much interested and Clay kept him well informed of the bill's progress.[33] He did hope that he could get enough support to force the Liberals to incorporate an examination in their bill. The Reform League took a very dim view of Clay's bill, condemning him for aiding the obstructionist tactics of the Tories.

The League was not generally pleased with Gladstone's bill either but refrained from criticizing it because the measure had some chance of succeeding. When, however, Robert Lowe and the old Palmerstonians completed their estrangement from the Liberals and condemned any reform as a threat to the constitution, the League expressed their support for Gladstone despite the shortcomings of his bill. On April 11, a meeting was held at St. Martin's Hall in London to express working class support for Gladstone's bill. To the amazement of most present, Lord Elcho, a leader of the Adullamites, rose to speak in support of Clay's despised bill. A vain and patronizing man, Elcho was convinced that government was the natural function of the wealthy and the aristocratic. Because he had been working throughout 1865 and 1866 to bring about a change in the Master and Servant Acts, Elcho had become well known in working class circles. He had managed to strike up a friendship with Holyoake in 1865 when Baines' motion was being debated.[34] One of Holyoake's great difficulties, whether in Secularism or in politics, was that he was always forming relationships with the wrong people. When Elcho began to speak, he was hissed by the throng of workingmen; he was allowed to continue for a short time after order was restored. On April 13, Elcho was surprised and the Reform Leaguers were stupified to read a letter in the *Times*, signed by G.J. Holyoake, offering a semi-official apology to Elcho from the League. Although he did not approve of Elcho's ideas, Holyoake commended him for his courage and frankness.[35] That a member of their governing council would publicly defend a man who had so often sneered at the working class and condemned democracy made the Leaguers and Parliamentary radicals very suspicious. Where exactly did Holyoake's sympathies lie?[36]

Gladstone's bill continued to have difficulty in Parliament as proposed amendments were defeated by increasingly narrow margins. Each day the Conservatives gained votes. Realizing that defections from the Liberal party had doomed the bill, Russell resigned on June 26, 1866. Lord Derby was called once again to form a government. Immediately upon Russell's resignation, the Reform League scheduled a demonstration. On June 29, ten thousand workingmen met at Trafalgar Square; they marched first to Gladstone's residence to cheer and then to Lord Elcho's to jeer him again. Radical M.P.s had also begun to build popular support for reform in their constituencies. Taking advantage of spontaneous enthusiasm, the League planned an even larger meeting for July 23 at Hyde Park—a royal park which the government had previously claimed the right to close to the public. The League's council was careful, however, to observe necessary legalities. A request was submitted to the Home Secretary, Spencer Walpole, to hold their rally at Hyde Park. Walpole forbade it but the League's council was not willing to accept his denial of their request. Edmond Beales favored abiding by Walpole's decision, but he was overruled by the

council, led on the issue by Bradlaugh.   The right to assemble on
public property was not to be denied.[37]

At 6:00 P.M. on July 23, the League officers, including
Holyoake and Bradlaugh, preceded a throng of twenty-thousand
workingmen to the gates of Hyde Park. After the police, who had
been dispatched by Sir Richard Mayne, the Metropolitan Police
Commissioner, refused their admission, Beales and the others
turned to leave satisfied that their rights had been asserted and that
the government had been sufficiently embarrassed. Because of the
large crowd, a section of the railings around the park collapsed and
a number of minor scuffles between the workingmen and police
ensued resulting in the arrest of numerous workingmen for
disorderly conduct.

The Hyde Park affair did not imply that the working class was
becoming more revolutionary; there was, however, the possibility
that the cooler heads in the Reform League would now be replaced
by those who counseled immediate even violent action against the
obstinate government. At this point, another instance of public
disorder would have done much to destroy the image of respectability which the working class had assumed. Lord Elcho and the
Adullamites had condemned workingmen as people of "venality,
ignorance and drunkeness."[38] How many more M.P.s frightened
by disorder in the streets, would have been disposed to accept such
outrageous rhetoric? The events of the next few days—a complicated
series of episodes between Walpole, the Reform League, and
Holyoake—allayed the fears of Conservatives while, at the same
time, prevented the League from provoking another confrontation
with the government.

On July 24, Beales and a deputation of the League which
included Holyoake returned to Walpole's office and demanded the
right to use Hyde Park for a mass meeting on the following Monday,
July 30. Walpole, a weak and indecisive bureaucrat—some accounts
report that he wept at this meeting—requested that Beales make his
request in writing in order that the entire cabinet could make this
decision. Beales and others present apparently believed that
Walpole had given them permission and that the written request
only served to fulfill a formality. Within a few hours of this
conference, London streets were flooded with handbills calling
workmen to another Hyde Park assembly. Whether this action by
the League was the result of a deliberate attempt to intimidate the
government or was really produced by a simple misunderstanding

may never by known. What likely happened was that Walpole had *not* made himself perfectly clear and that, at an informal meeting of the League's council later in the day, the decision was made to capitalize on an ambiguous situation. They knew that Walpole was not highly respected because he lacked decisiveness. If trouble did occur, he, and not the League, would bear the blame.

On the next day, July 25, Holyoake went to the Home Secretary's offices because he had been notified of another meeting with Walpole. Expecting to find the rest of the council and Walpole there, Holyoake was surprised when he found only Walpole's secretary. [39] Apparently, the League's secretary, George Howell, had failed to communicate a last minute change of plans. In any event, Holyoake did inform Spencer Walpole's secretary that it had been clearly understood that permission to use the parks had not been granted. How anyone could have been mistaken, Holyoake confessed, he did not know.[40] On July 26, Walpole was called before Parliament to relate why he had granted the League permission to rally in Hyde Park. Denying that he had done so, Walpole produced Holyoake's statement which his secretary had had the good sense to record. Beales and the League's council had departed from his office on the 24th knowing full well, Walpole asserted, that they had been denied the use of any royal park. A "misunderstanding," therefore, was a perfidious fabrication. To add credibility to Holyoake's testimony, Walpole acknowledged him to be "a most able member of the Reform League who is known to many members of this House." But the Home Secretary put the wrong construction on Holyoake's action and certainly increased the League's animosity toward Holyoake by adding that he had come to "repudiate in strongest terms Mr. Beales' proclamation." [41] Holyoake would never have intentionally disavowed the action of the Reform League to the Home Secretary. Beales, however, seemed to accept Walpole's description of Holyoake's motives. In a letter to the *Times* he publicly condemned Holyoake for becoming a willing accomplice of those elements in the government which sought to discredit the Reform League and to prevent franchise reform. [42] Confronted with the League's hostility, Holyoake could only reaffirm that he had, in all innocence, told the truth about the meeting with Walpole's secretary. [43] There is no reason to doubt him because, although he did not get along well with all members of the League's council, he would not have lied just to defend Walpole. At this point, however, nothing Holyoake could have said would have convinced the League that he had not committed an unforgiveable act of treachery.

The immediate outcome of these disclosures was that the League Council, not wishing to be charged with deliberate deceit, met on July 27, and relocated their meeting to the Agriculture Hall, Islington. It, therefore, took great courage for Holyoake to appear there. As he later confessed, had it not been for the company of John Stuart Mill, he might have experienced physical harm. At this noisy demonstration of working class solidarity, Beales and Bradlaugh were the main speakers. Before departing, the crowd resolved that agitation would cease only when Gladstone had been returned to office.[44] Little did they realize that franchise reform would be won before the Liberals could return.

On September 16, 1866, Lord Derby confided to Disraeli that he was "coming reluctantly to the conclusion that we shall have to deal with the question of Reform." [45] Since July, Parliamentary radicals and Reform League agitators had been holding numerous public meetings; continued delay in presenting a reform bill would only operate against the conservatives. Disraeli's decision to "dish the Whigs" and the actual progress of the bill he introduced in February 1867 constitute in the words of Robert Blake, "one of the oddest histories of confusion, cross-purposes and muddle in British political history." [46] Neither, we might add, is that story especially pertinent to Holyoake's life.

Actually, Holyoake's activities between August 1866 and August 1867 when the Second Reform Bill did become law are something of a mystery. He did anonymously edit a periodical, *The Working Man*, which, in addition to technical articles, featured columns of praise for Gladstone and the Liberals. One event, however, was particularly significant for both Holyoake and the League. John Bright had been campaigning vigorously, even threateningly, to turn the force of opinion into "an exhibition of another kind of force" if the Conservatives continued to ignore reform.[47] On December 3, 1866, Bright climaxed his campaign. Twenty-five thousand attended a London rally where Bright was joined on the platform by Beales, Holyoake, and by representatives of the moderate Reform Union, the thoroughly middle class heir of the Anti-Corn Law League. Holyoake had, by this time, apparently made his peace with Beales and the League. The alliance with the Reform Union indicates that the League intended to broaden its base of agitation.

After Disraeli introduced his bill in February 1867, the less moderate members of the League begged for a policy which would force the Conservatives to carry through with their promises. Once again the League chose to meet in Hyde Park. Walpole prohibited the demonstration but, on May 6, 1867, between 100,000 and 150,000 workingmen filed into the park there to be addressed by the League's council. Holyoake does not indicate that he was one of the speakers. Had he been present, it is most unlikely that he would have failed to record the event. In any case, May 6 was a day of complete victory for the League because the government made no attempt to disperse them. Walpole resigned in humiliation and Lord Derby admitted to Parliament that the government had "suffered some slight humiliation in the public mind." [48] The partisans of Reform had won a great victory partly because Disraeli had already set his course in the direction of reform and partly because the League had been prevented from prematurely forcing the issue.

On August 15, 1867, after parliamentary maneuvering had eliminated the fancy franchises from the Conservative measure, the Reform Bill became law. 900,000 potential voters were created nearly doubling the size of the electorate. Theoretically, the working class was now in the majority in many towns. There was no disorder and very little fear was now expressed about the future of the constitution. When Lord Derby spoke about "a leap in the dark," he did not intend to express fear for the future well-being of the realm. He was concerned rather about the composition of Parliament and about the method and cost of elections in the years to come. Party organization and election procedures were significantly altered because of the increased number of voters, but the House continued to remain a province of the wealthy. Rather than initiate a fundamental political readjustment, the Second Reform Bill testified to the economic and social progress made by urban workingmen since the early 1850s.

The radicals were not overly impressed with the bill; it did not embody manhood suffrage and it was not, as many of them realized, a direct result of their months of organized agitation. Holyoake, however, was very pleased with the bill and wrote to Disraeli thanking him for "the thought of the People-shown in the progress of the Reform Bill." He assured Disraeli that "the English people have a sense of order and gratitude . . . they will honor the minister who has opened it (the franchise) unto them." [49] But, as the general election of 1868 would reveal, Holyoake was quite wrong to promise the gratitude of the working classes to the Conservatives.

Now that urban laborers had finally received the franchise, Holyoake declared in August 1868 that voting must be made secret. Although the ballot had been part of the League's platform, some radicals, including Mill, believed that the secret ballot was "un-English". *A New Defence of the Ballot*, the third of Holyoake's political tracts, emphasized that the secret ballot was necessary if new electors were to be free of intimidation. In many counties, for example, the electorate was not yet large enough to provide the voter with anonymity. Rather than un-English, Holyoake believed the ballot represented traditional independence and defiance.[50] His pamphlet, highly commended by John and Jacob Bright, Gladstone, J.A. Roebuck and F.W. Newman, did help to keep an important issue under consideration.[51] In 1872 Gladstone's reforming ministry made the secret ballot a reality.

Because of ill health, Lord Derby resigned his office in February 1868; and Disraeli climbed finally to the "top of the greasy pole" to become the Prime Minister. Hardly had he taken office when his great rival, Gladstone, proposed that the Irish Church be disestablished. Disraeli declared that such a momentous question should be decided by a Parliament elected by the enlarged electorate. In the general election scheduled for October, Holyoake climaxed his political activities by offering himself for one of the Birmingham seats. "The object of my being a candidate at Birmingham," he wrote in his autobiography, "was to test and advocate the question of working class representation."[52] Perhaps this statement may be taken at face value but Holyoake must have realized that he had little chance to be elected in Birmingham because three strong Liberal candidates—George Dixon, P.H. Muntz, and John Bright—had already declared. Neither the Conservatives nor anyone else had a favorable opportunity to win a Birmingham contest.

In his address to the electors of Birmingham, October 16, 1868, later published as *Working Class Representation: Its Conditions and Consequences*, Holyoake called for the abolition of the Irish church, an end to pauperism, compulsory elementary education and the secret ballot. What he advocated was a rather standard Liberal program. Rather than promote his own candidacy, Holyoake chose to praise the qualities of Gladstone and the Birmingham Liberal candidates. Disraeli's role in bringing about franchise reform, Holyoake now characterized as nothing but a "splendid sin" which happened to have been committed in the interest of the people.[53]

There would come a day, prophesied Holyoake, when laboring men would find their way to Parliament. For the present, however, it would remain a "rich man's club." [54] The speech was hardly designed to generate much enthusiasm for his own candidacy. Holyoake was campaigning, not to garner the Birmingham working class vote for himself, but for the Liberal candidates. This judgement is substantiated by the fact that his campaign fund, £ 50, was provided indirectly from the Liberal party. [55]

The Liberal Chief Whip, G.C. Glynn, echoing Lord Derby, had warned Gladstone before the election, "All is new and changed and large and I fear I must say in some respects dark." [56] The Liberals did, however, have a plan for organizing the enlarged constituencies. The Reform League, of which six-hundred branches existed in 1867, had naturally lost much support after the Reform Bill had been passed. Not wishing to disband after partial victory, the League leaders—George Howell in particular—were desperately in need of funds to maintain their organizational apparatus. The League had always been somewhat dependent on Liberal politicians and manufacturers, such as Samuel Morley, for money. In return for grants to "special funds," administered quite secretly by Howell, the Liberal party received information which helped it to organize its election machinery. The League also supplied men, their expenses paid out of the Liberal donations which amounted to nearly £ 2,000, to travel throughout the country addressing working class clubs and unions. Working class candidates were not encouraged and were only given token amounts. According to the tone of his Birmingham address, Holyoake understood his mission very well.

The alliance with the League definitely contributed to the Liberal's victory: a majority of 112 seats in the House. With this mandate, Gladstone was able to carry on his own reform program—a most impressive counterpoint to Disraeli's victory of 1867. This agreement also initiated the Liberal-Labor alliance which lasted until the end of the century. Holyoake, of course, was defeated at Birmingham, but he never expected to win. Edmond Beales, Bradlaugh and Ernest Jones also were defeated after quite vigorous campaigns. For many years, independent labor representation would be an insignificant issue. [57] With the Liberals in firm control in 1868, the League quickly disintegrated.

Holyoake was now over fifty years old, but he appeared to be more vigorous than he had been for some time. Having played a minor yet active role in political developments, he turned now from politics to other activities: to Secularism briefly and to the cooperative movement which had been experiencing a quiet but vigorous growth for the last two prosperous decades. By 1869 the cooperative movement had re-emerged, revitalized and with considerably different objectives from the utopian schemes with which it had been concerned a generation before. Many of the men who had been active in communal activities of the 1840s were still to be found in the vanguard of the new cooperative movement. For the remainder of his life, into the twentieth century, Holyoake would be known as one of the foremost cooperators.

NOTES TO CHAPTER FIVE

[1] See John Vincent, *The Formation of the British Liberal Party* (New York: Charles Scribner's Sons, 1966), pp. 76-82 for a discussion of working class element of the Liberal Party.

[2] The most important recent published studies of the Reform Bill of 1867 are F.B. Smith, *The Making of the Second Reform Bill* (Cambridge, England: Cambridge University Press, 1966) and Maurice Cowling, *1867: Disraeli, Gladstone and Revolution* (Cambridge, England: Cambridge University Press, 1967). Joseph Park, *The English Reform Bill of 1867* (New York: Columbia University Press, 1920), for many years the standard work on the subject, is now superseded by Smith's narrative and by the impressive research of Professor Cowling. Further analyses of the bill and the events preceding it can be found in Gillespie, *Labour and Politics*, Simon Maccoby, *English Radicalism, 1853-1886;* Asa Briggs, *The Age of Improvement* and *Victorian People* both have the Reform Bill as their focal point. In Royden Harrison's *Before the Socialists*, Chapter II is especially pertinent. Finally, a student of the bill should not overlook Robert Blake, *Disraeli* (New York: Doubleday and Company, 1968).

[3] Although Joseph McCabe's biography discusses Holyoake's political life in the 1860's in considerable detail, the reference point is quite obscure.

[4] Smith, *The Making of the Second Reform Bill*, p.9. See also E.J. Hobsbawm, *Labouring Men* (New York: Doubleday and Company, 1967), pp. 321-70. The status of their income, the regularity of their employment and the nature of their occupation made the labor aristocracy a well-defined group.

[5] Michael Packe, *Orsini* (Boston: Little, Brown and Company, 1957), pp. 240-41, 249. See also Holyoake, *Sixty Years*, II, 326-32. The account in his autobiography reveals that Holyoake viewed his "experiments" as something of a lark and not as part of a deadly plot.

[6] *Reasoner*, XXIII, No. 9 (1858), 71.

[7] G.M. Trevelyan, *The Life of John Bright* (London: Constable and Co., Ltd., 1913), p. 271. Herman Ausubel, *John Bright: Victorian Reformer* (New York: John Wiley and Sons, Inc. 1966) in no way supersedes Trevelyan's masterful biography.

[8] Holyoake, *The Workman and the Suffrage* (London: Holyoake and Company, 1858), p. 5.

[9] *Ibid.*, p. 7.

[10] Samuel Smiles, *Self-Help* (London: John Murray, 1958). This edition commemorates the 100th anniversary of Smiles' popular book. See Asa Briggs' informative comments on self-help in the introduction, pp. 7-31.

[11] Blake, *Disraeli*, p. 381. See also, Smith, *The Making of the Second Reform Bill*, pp. 39-44.

[12] The *Times* (London), March 22, 1859, p. 6.

[13] Quoted in Llewellyn Woodward, *The Age of Reform* (Oxford: The Clarendon Press, 1962), p. 169.

[14] Bonner, *Charles Bradlaugh*, I, 219.

[15] Sir John Trelawny to Holyoake (March 1, 1861), No. 1288 and (February 17, 1863), No. 1470, C.U.

[16] Briggs, *Victorian People*, p. 179.

[17] McCabe, *Life and Letters of Holyoake*, I, 307-33 contains a lengthy discussion of the Garibaldi Legion and Holyoake's role in getting it to Italy. The Minute Book of the committee is contained in the Holyoake Collection, Bishopsgate Institute.

[18] Holyoake, *Bygones Worth Remembering*, I, 255.

[19] Gillespie, *Labor and Politics*, p. 219.

[20] John Stuart Mill to Holyoake (April 28, 1865) No. 1594, C.U.

[21] Holyoake, *The Liberal Situation: Necessity for a Qualified Franchise* (London: London Bookstore, 1865), p. 14.

[22] Great Britain, *Hansard's Parliamentary Debates*, 3rd series, Vol. 178 (May 3, 1865), c. 1429.

[23] *Ibid.*, (May 8, 1865), c. 1617.

[24] *Ibid.*, c. 1621.

[25] Quoted in Gillespie, *Labor and Politics*, p. 251.

[26] Cowling, *1867: Disraeli, Gladstone and Revolution*, p. 3.

[27] Edward Mack and W.H.G. Armytage, *Thomas Hughes* (London: Ernest Benn Ltd., 1952), pp. 144-146.

[28] Joseph Cowen Jr. to Holyoake (Oct. 24, 1862), No. 1448, C.U. and W.E. Gladstone to Holyoake (Oct. 20, 1862), No. 1447, C.U.

[29] Phillip Magnus, *Gladstone* (New York: E.P. Dutton and Company, 1964), p. 170.

[30] Smith, *The Making of the Second Reform Bill*, pp. 50-120 contains a complete discussion of the provisions of Gladstone's bill of 1866.

[31] George Howell, Secretary of the Reform League, to Holyoake (February 20, 1866), No. 1649, C.U.

[32] Quoted in Smith, *Making of the Second Reform Bill*, p. 63.

[33] James Clay to Holyoake, (March 12, 1866), No. 1653, C.U. and (March 23, 1866), No. 1655, C.U.

[34] Holyoake to Elcho (May 17, 1865), No. 1603, C.U. and Elcho to Holyoake (May 19, 1865), No. 1604, C.U. An illuminating discussion of Elcho's character and influence is presented by Daphne Simon, "Master and Servant," *Democracy and the Labour Movement*, ed. John Saville (London: Laurence & Wishart, Ltd., 1954).

[35] The *Times* (London), April 13, 1866, p. 12. See also Lord Elcho to Holyoake, (April 13, 1866), No. 1665, C.U.

[36] P.A. Taylor to Holyoake (April 13, 1866), No. 1667, C.U.

[37] Smith, *The Making of the Second Reform Bill*, p. 128.

[38] Anthony Wood, *Nineteenth Century Britain* (London: McKay, 1960), p. 272.

[39] Holyoake, *Sixty Years*, II, 493-497 contains a complete account of his version of this adventure.

[40] The *Times* (London), July 27, 1866, p. 5 and *Hansard*, 3rd series Vol. 184 (July 29, 1866), c. 1491-1494.

[41] *Hansard*, Vol. 184 (July 26, 1866) c. 1494. See also Holyoake to Walpole (July 27, 1866), No. 1680; Walpole to Holyoake (July 29, 1866), No. 1682; and Walpole to Holyoake (July 30, 1866), No. 1638, C.U. For

Walpole's version of this affair, see S.W. Walpole, *The History of Twenty-Five Years* (London: Longmans, Green and Co., 1904), II, 170-76.

[42] The *Times* (London), July 18, 1866, p. 9.

[43] *Ibid.*, July 30, 1866, p. 13.

[44] *Ibid.*, July 31, 1866, p. 3.

[45] Quoted in Blake, *Disraeli*, p. 433.

[46] *Ibid.*, p. 438.

[47] Smith, *The Making of the Second Reform Bill*, p. 141.

[48] Quoted in Harrison, *Before the Socialists*, p. 96. See the *Times* (London), May 6, 1867, pp. 8-9; and May 7, 1867, p. 9, for further accounts of the demonstration and the government's response.

[49] Quoted in McCabe, *Life and Letters of Holyoake*, II, 36.

[50] Holyoake, *A New Defence of the Ballot* (London: Bookstore, 1868), p. 5.

[51] John Bright to Holyoake, (August 21, 1868), No. 1813; Jacob Bright to Holyoake (August 15, 1868), No. 1810; Gladstone to Holyoake (August 15, 1868), No. 1819; and F.W. Newman to Holyoake, (August 24, 1868), No. 1816, C.U.

[52] Holyoake, *Sixty Years*, II, 458.

[53] Holyoake, *Working Class Representation: Its Conditions and Consequences* (Birmingham: Guest, 1868), p. 7.

[54] *Ibid.*, p. 8.

[55] Somerset Beaumont to Holyoake (October 4, 1868); No. 1826, C.U. See Harrison, *Before the Socialists*, pp. 137-209 and also Royden Harrison "The British Working Class and the General Election of 1868," *International Review of Social History*, VI (1961), 75.

[56] Harrison, *Before the Socialists*, p. 137. Harrison has made a painstaking analysis of Liberal party and Reform League records to produce his important studies of the 1868 elections.

[57] Writing to Karl Marx on November 18, 1868, Engels complained that "Everywhere the proletariat is the tag, rag and bobtail of the official parties." Quoted in Harrison, "The British Working Class and the General Election," *IRSH*, VI (1961), p. 87.

CHAPTER VI

THE COOPERATIVE MOVEMENT 1867 — 1879

"I have cared more for cooperation than for any other movement in which I have engaged." These words, spoken by Holyoake near the end of his life, are inscribed on a monument erected by his fellow cooperators. From 1869 until his death in 1906, Holyoake was an enthusiastic cooperator and, although his contribution to the development of organized cooperation was less than that made by other men, he did supply the cooperative movement with his skill as a journalist. More importantly, Holyoake, E.V. Neale, Lloyd Jones, E.O. Greening, William Pare and other men who had been Owenites or Christian Socialists brought their idealism and hard-gained experience to a younger generation which also had great hopes that mutual aid would mitigate an insecure economic situation. The great boom of mid-century was subsiding and, as foreign manufacturers began to recapture their share of markets, production and wage levels in Britain began to stabilize. British workingmen then turned to their trade unions and cooperative societies to insure that their economic gains of the past two decades would not be lost.

British cooperative history divides into three phases. First, there was the Owenite or utopian period which met a sad conclusion at Queenwood. The second phase inauspiciously began in August 1844 at the Lancashire village of Rochdale. Faced with depression and with technological unemployment, a handful of Rochdale weavers initiated yet another cooperative solution for their economic plight. Christening themselves the Rochdale Society of Equitable Pioneers, thirty-four men—the majority of whom were disillusioned Owenites —assumed the task of constructing a society which embodied "arrangements for the pecuniary benefit, and improvement of the social and domestic condition of its members."[1]

Although they initially retained the hope of eventually establishing a colony, the Rochdale Pioneers conducted a thoroughly

practical society. First they established a store in which basic
commodities were retailed. The venture proved to be an immediate
success. Cooperators had previously been more anxious to establish
producer associations or labor exchanges. Entirely accepting the
labor theory of value, earlier cooperators attempted to construct
institutions through which a laborer might receive a price equal to
the value of the produce which embodied his labor. By their concern
with distribution rather than production, the Rochdale Pioneers
evidenced their accommodation to capitalism; and they established
the guidelines upon which other cooperatives would be created.
Because the extension of credit to the cooperative's members was
strictly forbidden, the possibility of financial disaster was greatly
reduced. In the past many societies had been ruined because the
usually humanitarian cooperators had often heeded the pleas of
indigent members. The most novel and attractive of Rochdale's
innovations was the provision that each member receive a quarterly
dividend in proportion to the amount of purchases he had made
from the store. Heretofore, cooperatives had either placed profits in
a colonization fund, or as was most often the case, allowed profits to
be dissipated by loans; now each member was to receive a share of
surplus revenue.

Beginning in 1844 with capital assets of only £ 28, the society
grew slowly until the late 1840's. In 1849 the Rochdale Savings Bank
failed and the small savings of many Rochdale workingmen were
lost. A considerable number of them now began to invest in the
Rochdale Pioneers because the society promised to engage in no
credit activity and because the "divi" was a convenient way of
increasing one's savings. Moreover, the retail store's prices were no
more than those charged by other establishments. From 140
members with a capital of £ 397 in 1848, the Rochdale society
mushroomed to a membership of 600 with a combined investment of
£ 2,300 in 1850. (See Table A for a summary of Rochdale's amazing
progress over the years). Retailing and savings programs were not,
however, the only function of the Rochdale cooperators. The able
guidance given the society by men such as Abraham Greenwood
stressed a diversified program. They invested in a cornmill society
and in a manufacturing society; a day school was also established.
By the early 1850s Rochdale's success was acknowledged throughout Great Britain.

By their example, the Rochdale Pioneers gave new courage to
other cooperators, and the prosperity which began in the early

TABLE A

THE ROCHDALE PIONEERS *

Year	Membership	Capital	Sales	Profits and Interest
		£	£	£
1844	28	28	-	-
1846	80	252	1147	81
1848	140	397	2276	118
1850	600	2300	13180	890
1855	1400	11033	44903	3106
1860	3450	37710	152063	15906
1865	5326	78778	196234	25156
1870	5566	80291	223021	25209
1875	8415	225682	305657	48212
1880	10613	292570	283655	48545

* Cole, *A Century of Cooperation*, p. 81

1850s made possible the establishment of similar societies; it is estimated that in 1851 approximately 130 cooperatives were in existence. [3] The transition from "community building to shopkeeping" was assuredly beginning to take place. [4] More frequently, cooperators echoed the words recorded by William Smith of Bridgnorth: "We have seen enough of Utopian ridiculous mummery of Socialism . . . We don't want it; we have seen the new moral world and don't like it . . . ." [5] During the 1850's as real wages rose especially for skilled laborers, the incentive to organize cooperatives did not decline. Several important developments transpired in these years which were to prove of great importance after the rate of British industrial expansion began to slacken in the late 1860s.

The future of cooperation was assured in 1852 by the passage of the Industrial and Provident Societies Act. Credited principally to the lobbying activities of E.V. Neale and the Christian Socialists, this act permitted a society to raise capital for any legal purpose including any productive enterprise except mining. Although the Christian Socialists and their workingmen's association did not survive, the legislation which they procured from Parliament certainly did assist the cooperative movement. Even small societies could now legally raise funds sufficient to purchase goods in quantity directly from the manufacturer and to retail these same goods at near wholesale prices. Cooperatives could attract a greater number of members because their stores could offer very competitive prices. According to the desire of the membership, profits could either be distributed or plowed back into the society for further investments.

One serious limitation to cooperative progress continued to exist, however, because the Industrial and Provident Societies Act did not permit societies to pool their resources or transfer capital to a central agency. Abraham Greenwood, Lloyd Jones and Henry Pitman, editor of the *Cooperator* magazine, petitioned Parliament in the late 1850s to amend the Industrial and Provident Societies Act in such a way that individual cooperatives could combine their holdings. In 1862 this action was taken, thus making a cooperative federation entirely possible. The following year, eight societies joined to form the North of England Wholesale and Industrial Provident Society (hereafter referred to as the "C.W.S."). Abraham Greenwood was elected president; from this time, the cooperative movement progressed steadily toward becoming a national venture.

During the 1850s Holyoake had become more than passively

interested in cooperation, devoting an increasing amount of space in the *Reasoner* to cooperative progress. In 1858—that year of Secularist crisis and of the beginning of his political involvement—Holyoake wrote *Self-Help by the People*, a history of the Rochdale Pioneers. Because it embodied the Victorian formula for success and because of the society's fame, this little book became one of Holyoake's most noteworthy publications. The Rochdale men, he asserted, had profited because they had independently managed their affairs and because they had developed "provident habits." In a short time they had learned what "forty years of competition had failed to teach other men." [6] As a historical account, Holyoake's narrative was flawed by inaccuracies. "It has been said," wrote the secretary of the Rochdale society, "that in some places in your history, movements that took place at different times appear as if they occurred simultaneously." [7] It received considerable acclaim, however, from the *Westminster Review*, the *Economist*, and the *New York Daily Tribune*. [8] In following years, *Self-Help by the People* was translated into French, Spanish, Italian, German and Hungarian; it had also to be acknowledged that several cooperatives had been founded by men who had been made aware of the potential of cooperation by Holyoake's history. [9]

Although he had never shown much interest in Secularist federation, Holyoake was much attracted by the idea of a national cooperative organization because of its obvious financial advantages. After 1863 he wholeheartedly supported the CWS. Rapid progress did, however, have its disadvantages. Many men were drawn into the movement who had little appreciation for the sacrifices made by an earlier generation of cooperators. As did other cooperative veterans, Holyoake believed that the movement would be poorer if all the ideals were forsaken. Too much stress, he believed, was being placed upon the "divi" and too little attention given to the essential nature of cooperation. In 1863 Holyoake wrote two pamphlets in which he complained that cooperators were coming dangerously close to repeating the mistakes which had contributed to earlier failures. *Moral Errors which Endanger the Permanence of Cooperative Societies* was a condemnation of the excessive concern which individual cooperators displayed for their little profits. Competing with one another like petty capitalists for greater dividends could lead, Holyoake warned, to their mutual destruction. [10]

In a second tract, A *"Working Man's" Objections to Coopera-*

tive Societies Answered, Holyoake raised a fundamentally theoretical issue for cooperators, many of whom had been taught that all behavior, including economic activity, was based upon the pursuit of self-interest. How could true cooperation ever succeed when everyone involved was naturally competitive? Holyoake maintained that cooperation did not seek to frustrate self-interest but to harness this drive more closely to the utilitarian test of all action. Declaring that the liberal economic regulator, the "unseen hand," had proven to be a dangerous fiction, Holyoake stressed that cooperation was built upon enlightened reason which led to concerted action. Therefore, the greatest good, both private and public, could be achieved in terms of cooperation. [11]

The next stage of Holyoake's involvement in cooperation began after his foray into politics at the time of the Second Reform Bill. Walter Morrison, M.P., who was much interested in cooperation, approached Holyoake and E.O. Greening, editor of the *Industrial Partnership's Record,* about the possibility of publishing a new cooperative journal. Henry Pitman's *Cooperator* was the only journal which systematically advocated the formation of a national cooperative organization. Because the *Cooperator* was in serious financial difficulties, Morrison believed that a new journal was needed to maintain local interest in the federation. If Greening and Holyoake consented to assume the task, Morrison promised to guarantee them financial support to the tune of £300. [12] Beginning the *Social Economist* in March 1868 and continuing to August 1869, Holyoake, often writing under the pseudonym of "Landor Praed," and Greening reported what cooperative progress was being made. The day of a truly national cooperative movement was not far distant.

On August 28, 1868, E.V. Neale presided over a preliminary conference from which the announcement was issued that a London cooperative congress would be held the following February. Invited to participate were representatives of cooperative stores, manufacturing societies, trade unions and individuals who were especially interested in the cooperative movement. The agenda for the meeting, as reported by the *Social Economist,* included a definition of the relationship between the cooperative movement and the trade unions, discussion of methods for promoting general interest in cooperation, and the means by which cooperative societies might unite. [13] Neale received very few acknowledgements, however, potential delegates having their attention diverted perhaps by the general election held in October; the February conference was, therefore, cancelled.

In March 1869 William Pare, a man long active in socialist and cooperative affairs (once the registrar of Birmingham before he was dismissed for his association with Owen, Pare had officiated at Holyoake's marriage in 1840), issued a call for a similar congress. This time, better plans were made; a committee which included many prestigious names was created to arrange for a cooperative congress to be held in London at the end of May. Headed by Thomas Hughes, this committee included Holyoake, Robert Applegarth, Louis Blanc, W.S. Jevons, Kingsley, Ludlow, John Stuart Mill and E.V. Neale. Walter Morrison and Greening served as co-treasurers while William Pare took the secretarial duties upon himself. Convened on May 31, the London Cooperative Congress was attended by representatives of fifty-seven British cooperative societies. Although the conveners were not, with a few exceptions such as Greening, active cooperators, they were men long interested in cooperation.[14] The truly working class element was nevertheless very strong and growing, especially in the north of England. The assembled delegates resolved to act jointly whenever possible with the trade unions, to establish an exchange between producer cooperatives, to hold a cooperative exhibition, to seek the creation of a cooperation credit association and to establish a central committee to coordinate and implement these and future resolutions.[15]

Although the conference was generally uneventful, one of the few controversial issues occurred when Holyoake presented a resolution for the creation of a London Cooperative Board to facilitate communication between cooperatives in the north of England and in Scotland with the London cooperators.[16] J.M. Ludlow opposed this resolution on the grounds that county boards should be organized first and a national convention held before any central board or committee could legitimately function. Otherwise, Ludlow argued, it would appear that the Londoners were trying to place themselves in a too prestigious position. A provisional committee composed of sixteen men, including Neale, Hughes, Applegarth, Greening, Jones, Ludlow, Pare and Holyoake, was established as Holyoake had recommended. Their sole purpose was to establish a stronger sense of unity between the CWS, the Scottish Cooperative Wholesale Society and London. Although no national cooperative organization had been established at this congress, the machinery necessary to foster a greater sense of unity had been brought into existence.

At the second Cooperative Congress held at Manchester in June 1870, the Cooperative Union Ltd. was founded and the third phase of cooperation was officially begun. Each cooperative which joined the Union was required to remit one penny per member to finance the operation of a central committee. An appeal to join was distributed to 750 societies and, although only 183 responded, the £ 200 subscribed was sufficient to hire William Nuttall, an accountant for the CWS, as a part-time executive secretary. Besides the founding of the Union, the most interesting feature of this congress was the accord between Lloyd Jones and Holyoake—old enemies who seldom found themselves in agreement on any subject. Jones voiced the complaint that present day cooperators seemed interested only in their dividends; his opinion was seconded by Holyoake who lamented the absence of the "stirring addresses" once delivered by men like Jones and William Pare. "If the old Cooperators erred in sentiment," Holyoake told the assembly, "certainly the present ones err in the direction of materialism." [17] As a result of these pronouncements, the delegates authorized the Union to establish a cooperative newspaper to replace the ephemeral cooperative journals. If each cooperator received a subscription, then something might be done to infuse the movement with the higher ideals which had animated cooperators in the past. In 1871 the *Cooperative News,* which has remained the organ of the Cooperative Union ever since, was founded.

Even though Holyoake was now very engrossed in cooperative activity, he was still able to be drawn back into the turbulent world of the National Secular Society. Since 1866 when the NSS had been officially founded, Charles Bradlaugh had enjoyed undisputed control over the membership. But Secularism was still identified with George Jacob Holyoake in the eyes of the general public. It is also true that some Secularists had retained Holyoake's ideas of the nature of their organization. In May 1870 Holyoake accepted Bradlaugh's offer to discuss their views in the form of an open debate. Austin Holyoake, now the assistant editor of the *National Reformer,* was chosen to moderate. The first proposition over which they contended was that "The Principles of Secularism do not include Atheism" with Holyoake naturally defending the affirmative position. On the second evening of their highly publicized and well-attended debate, Holyoake argued that "Secular Criticism does not involve Scripture" while Bradlaugh maintained, of course, that the real work of the Secularist was to attack religion.[18] Neither man departed from his previously stated position regarding the nature of Secularism, but Bradlaugh, hoping to use the debate to unify the Secular party, was careful not to antagonize Holyoake by being overly argumentative.

Bradlaugh did believe that their debate had served to minimize points of difference. Therefore, in September 1870 Bradlaugh requested Holyoake to join the ranks of the NSS as a vice president.[19] Holyoake replied, however, that "since the Secular Society upon whose behalf you write inculcates that Atheism is identical with Secularism, I could not take the office of Vice President in it without confusing the public mind as to the essential difference between Secularism and Atheism which I deem it so important to keep clear."[20] The finality of this statement is misleading for it actually served as a preface to Holyoake's greater activity in Secularism. He received the encouragement to do so, not from Bradlaugh, but from his fellow cooperators.

The more enthusiastic followers of Bradlaugh displayed no interest in the cooperative movement. Although the *National Reformer* did include some news of cooperative affairs, the militant Secularists confined themselves to anti-religious chores. Within the cooperative movement, however, there were those who were interested in Secularism and who believed that Holyoake still had a contribution to make. In October 1870 Holyoake received a request from thirty-two cooperators and Secularists, led by William Nuttall, to revive the *Reasoner*. A *Reasoner* Publishing Company was immediately created and a guarantee given Holyoake that he would receive half of all profits for his editorial services.[21] In Lancashire and Yorkshire, Secularism and the cooperative movement were most clearly associated; it was in these regions that most support for a new *Reasoner* existed.[22] Bradlaugh had apparently committed the same error as had Holyoake in the 1850s. By concentrating his attention on London, he had created resentment in the north. At one time, this area had produced the followers of Robert Cooper and Bradlaugh; now, they supported Holyoake.

While Holyoake was considering this offer, he chanced a visit to Glasgow. He found there that the city hall, in which he had once been able to lecture freely, was closed to all Secularists because of the offensive nature of Bradlaugh's recent speeches. He hesitated no longer and in January 1871 began again to edit the *Reasoner*. Subtitled "A Secular and Cooperative Review," the *Reasoner* was issued monthly until July 1872, and was devoted to restating

Holyoake's view of the nature of Secularism and to advertising cooperative affairs. "It is the first duty of a Secular Society to keep itself clear of the charge of Atheism," Holyoake wrote in his opening editorial.[23] Although he claimed that cooperation and Secularism were separate movements, Holyoake openly acknowledged that cooperators were financing the *Reasoner* and that it was their belief that cooperation was a true form of Secular activity.[24] At a time when many cooperators were concerned about excessive materialism, Secularism seemed to provide a restorative emphasis on duty and mutual concern. There is no way to determine how many cooperators considered themselves to be Secularists; but it is likely that the new *Reasoner* did circulate more among cooperators than among those Secularists who were not members of cooperative societies.

Meanwhile, the progress made by cooperators continued. The third congress, held at Birmingham in April 1871, continued the organizational development of the Cooperative Union. The central board was divided into a London section and a provincial section, an arrangement which continued until 1873 when five separate boards were created representing different geographical regions, the London section being then renamed the Southern section. Two representatives from each area were selected to constitute a united board which carried out the resolutions of the annual cooperative congresses and supervised the publishing of the *Cooperative News*. By 1873 the Cooperative Union had achieved a workable balance between centralized operation and local control exercised by the five regional boards.

The most significant reasons for the growth of British cooperation in these years were its practical aims. As defined in 1871 by the *Cooperative News*, cooperation was a moderate movement: "At present, it simply enables workingmen to save money, by economizing the distribution of wealth and dispensing with many of the middlemen who have been used to living by taking articles from the producer or wholesale dealer and handing them at an advanced price to the consumer."[25] According to this definition, cooperation existed simply to satisfy the needs of its affiliates. Holyoake, however, was not completely satisified with this definition especially as it was applied to the manufacturing or producer cooperatives. For what purposes, he asked, did they exist?

At the 1873 congress, Holyoake did attempt to impress upon cooperators a heightened sense of their public responsibility.

Addressing himself specifically to the producer cooperatives, he urged that not only should their workers receive a share of the profits but also that the customer receive consideration in the distribution of revenue. [26] Consumption, as economists were recognizing in the 1870s, was an indispensable concomitant to production. Cooperators must recognize, Holyoake had written before the conference, that "the service of the public is the aim of cooperation." [27] It is unclear what Holyoake meant when he insisted that profits be shared with consumers; perhaps he intended that a type of rebate system be introduced whereby the customer, according to the quantity of his purchases, would receive a return on the purchase price. Whatever he actually meant, Holyoake's contention that producer cooperatives take greater concern for their customers raised a minor row at the congress.

In the opinion of J.M. Ludlow, Holyoake's concern for the customer was excessive. He knew that consumption was essential to continuing production, but Ludlow also believed it of a secondary or "animalistic" order compared with the creative or "divine" nature of production.[28] By placing such emphasis on the consumer, Ludlow argued, Holyoake was actually exalting competition rather than cooperation. If the real concern of the manufacturer were to aid the public, would not the producer cooperatives degenerate to a state where they competed with one another by offering various plans to attract buyers? Rather than exalting competition, Holyoake was really trying to instill a greater degree of social consciousness in the producer cooperatives because he feared that cooperatives were becoming similar to joint stock companies.

In a second pamphlet published in 1873, *The Policy of Commercial Cooperation*, Holyoake presented his final reply to Ludlow, accusing him of holding ideas which were quite alien to the true spirit of cooperation. "The lode line of my argument," wrote Holyoake, "is that complete cooperation reaches the community and in such respect as any form of it falls short of that limit, it is mere competition under a disguised name." [29] Holyoake's idealism may have been laudable, but to request the producer cooperatives, many of which were threatened by failure because of declining markets in the 1870s, to share their profits was hardly feasible. Because the cooperative movement was primarily composed of consumer cooperatives, this controversy between Ludlow and Holyoake was of little practical importance. Both men had long been interested in cooperation and both were expressing a negative reaction to a situation in which profits and dividends received the greatest attention.

By being thoroughly practical, consumer's cooperation was able to survive. Although the more experienced cooperators were cheered by success, they found it difficult to appreciate the lack of an ideology of cooperation. The old Owenites and Christian Socialists had hoped that cooperators of a younger generation would retain something of the old moral world. The memory of Owen and patriarchs still living like Pare and Holyoake continued to be revered, but the concerns of the average cooperator lay mainly with percentages of profit and return on purchases. Those men, like Holyoake, who continued to look with some nostalgia to the past did not totally deplore the emphasis on profit because the cooperative movement was indeed the child of their creation; they did, however, continuously maintain that true progress was more than an adequately filled workingman's purse. What cooperation needed most in the 1870s was a sense of its past. Holyoake, therefore, intended to make cooperators more aware of their history.

*****

In the spring of 1872, Holyoake had announced that he was beginning a history of the cooperative movement. But during the next three years his work was frequently interrupted. John Stuart Mill died in August 1873 and all radicals paused to pay their respects. Mill had been Britain's great apostle of self-help, wrote Holyoake in the *Cooperative News*, an intellectual giant who taught the workingman to think independently and to gain his own liberty. [30] The following April, Holyoake was saddened by the death of his brother, Austin, but he continued to work on his history, relying mainly on his own recollections and those of others involved in the earlier years of cooperative activity.

Unfortunately, toward the end of 1874, illness struck Holyoake once again and by December he was completely blind. The publication of the first volume of his history was delayed although Holyoake had nearly completed working on the book. Believing that Holyoake's career was now finished, Walter Morrison and other cooperators immediately sought to provide him with some financial security for his old age. [31] Soon, over £2000 was collected; £500 was granted to Holyoake and an £ 100 annuity was purchased with the remainder. Cooperators, Secularists including Bradlaugh and even several prominent clergymen joined in this charitable tribute. Throughout the spring and early summer of 1875, Holyoake remained incapacitated while cooperators awaited the publication of the first volume of their history.

In July the volume dealing with cooperative activity from 1812 to 1844 was finally released. It was a disappointment; cooperators, as Joseph McCabe indicates, found the book "good reading but indifferent history." [32] Holyoake can not be much faulted because he was not a historian and he labored under the burden of ill health. He frequently failed to observe chronology and he often filled his book either with bland summations or with biased anecdotes about people with whom he had been associated in the early days of socialism whether or not their particular roles had been of much significance. Some cooperators were highly and justifiably critical of Holyoake's lack of objectivity. Lloyd Jones, for example, was lampooned as "Mr. Swearatonce" for taking the oath of Protestant orthodoxy in the 1840s. [33]

In the judgment of the *Cooperative News*, Holyoake's *History* placed too much emphasis on religious heresy. [34] Holyoake's own experiences understandably led him to make this identification. Cooperators in the 1870s, however, either did not believe that the religious aspects of Owenism had been especially significant or, if they were Christians, they were not pleased to read that the man whom they revered had achieved his greatest significance as a free-thinker. Holyoake claimed, somewhat inconsistently after his statements about Jones, that Owen had seriously damaged the cooperative cause by condemning Christianity, a criticism of Owen which reversed the opinion he and Southwell had maintained some thirty years before. To many readers, it seemed as if Holyoake had used his history in order to have the last word with old adversaries. The problem was that they were not yet dead or, in the case of Owen, had able defenders. In October 1875 Henry Travis, Owen's literary executor, passed damning judgment on the *History of Cooperation*. Owen had been so badly misrepresented, Travis claimed, that his admirers were sorry to see the book published. [35]

Negative criticism did not deter Holyoake from proceeding with the second volume. Toward the end of 1875, Holyoake began to recover his sight and vitality. Before the second volume could be completed, however, he had once again become embroiled in

Secularist affairs. One of Bradlaugh's young disciples, G.W. Foote, had become convinced that the NSS needed to do more than condemn Christianity. He also hoped to wrest the leadership away from Bradlaugh. In order to gain support, Foote enlisted the still feeble Holyoake to assist him in editing the *Secularist*, the intent of which, Holyoake explained, was to "refrain from discussing atheism as part of Secularism."[36] Just beginning to recover from his illness—Holyoake delivered his first lecture in several years on January 9, 1876—he did not devote much energy to this journal.

Holyoake soon surmised, after articles of which he disapproved appeared in the *Secularist*, that Foote was using him to advance his own future in the NSS. Immediately, he resigned his duties and expressed his indignation toward Foote in the *National Reformer*. By changing sides so abruptly, Holyoake actually exacerbated Secularist troubles because Bradlaugh and Foote both contended that the other was manipulating Holyoake, "stricken by old age and many infirmities," to advance a partisan cause.[37] Holyoake found Bradlaugh on this occasion to be very sympathetic; he also was reminded that the *National Reformer* had carried appeals for his annuity fund. Therefore, it is not completely surprising that on June 4, 1876, Holyoake was seated on the speaker's platform at the NSS conference in Leeds. Against the challenge of Foote, Bradlaugh was re-elected president; as his first act, he proposed to the conference that Holyoake be given a vice-presidency in the society. Holyoake accepted, admitting that his differences with Bradlaugh had now been completely reconciled.[38] Although he did assume the office, there is no record that Holyoake took part in any deliberations. The National Secular Society was badly fragmented and we may interpret Holyoake's acceptance of office as his attempt to restore some unity. Holyoake did have great respect for Bradlaugh's ability as a leader but he still wanted to infuse an element of toleration in Secularism.

In August 1876 Holyoake began to publish the *Secular Review*, a journal which he hoped would restore unity to the society. In February 1877 he made the mistake of turning the proprietorship of the paper over to Charles Watts, a man who cared little for Bradlaugh. Watts, in turn, joined with Foote in June 1877 to publish the *Secular Review and Secularist* which advocated the foundation of a completely new society, the British Secular Union. Because this society comprehended a non-atheistic Secularism, Holyoake commended it, but he did not actively join in its support.[39] The truth is that he no longer found any satisfaction in the movement to which he had contributed so much or in the journalistic squabbling in which he had engaged so often. Believing the differences between the rival conceptions of Secularism irreconcilable, he certainly would have agreed with the observation of one chronicler of Secularism who wrote: "Is the theoretical attack (on Christianity) really necessary or advisable? That was the problem which did more than any other single factor to split the ranks. Roughly speaking, Holyoake said No, Bradlaugh, Yes."[40] Holyoake quietly turned all of his attention back to the cooperative movement, excusing himself to both Secular parties on the grounds that the *History of Cooperation* demanded his full attention.

Regardless of criticism, Holyoake had become known as the historian of the cooperative movement. Beginning in November 1876 and continuing into 1877, he wrote over thirty lengthy articles for the *Cooperative News* serializing the history of the Rochdale Pioneers between 1857 and 1877. All the while, he continued to work as a member of the Southern section of the Cooperative Union and to collect data for the second volume of cooperative history. In early 1879 it was published and, like its predecessor, was neither objective nor accurate. E.V. Neale commended it but also indicated that readers should note Holyoake's biases and chronological lapses.[41] During 1879 and continuing into 1880, the *Cooperative News* received a number of irate letters—the majority written by Lloyd Jones—condemning the *History of Cooperation* for its failure to present a more balanced account. Had not Holyoake become such a revered person, the reaction to his history might have been even less polite. Most cooperators recognized that Holyoake's biases resulted from his close association with cooperation and his unfortunate experiences of the early 1840s. Therefore, his work was not altogether discredited and some years later he was commissioned to write histories of the Leeds Industrial Provident Society and the Derby Cooperative Society Ltd.

Happy to have completed his work, Holyoake made plans for a holiday abroad. In August 1879 he was able to fulfill a long standing ambition; Holyoake set out for the United States. He was given a complimentary dinner in Manchester on August 10 and another in Liverpool on August 15, the day before he departed for America. On August 28, Holyoake arrived in New York.[42] His main intention was to enjoy the adventure of travel, but because so many cooperators were interested in emigrating to the United States,

Holyoake had declared that he would try, as he traveled, to write a sort of guide book for emigrants. American cooperators, former British citizens, and freethinkers such as Robert Ingersoll attended to Holyoake, and the veteran radical thoroughly enjoyed his surprising acclaim. "You have lived," wrote Ingersoll to Holyoake, "a brave and useful life. You have broken many chains. You have lightened the burdens of the poor and in a thousand ways added to the blessings of mankind."[43]　After eight days in New York, he went to Boston where, on September 8, he delivered a speech to the Homestead Cooperative Savings Association. Everywhere he was asked to speak. Certainly this cordial reception helped to give Holyoake a favorable impression of the United States. He regularly submitted encouraging reports to the *Cooperative News* on the possibilities of emigration. On September 29, for example, he predicted that "America will become a new refuge for English industry as it once was for English freedom."[44]　From the East he traveled to Buffalo, to Cincinnati and as far west as Chicago. Holyoake was amazed at the pace of activity in the U.S. and at the total lack of deference shown by citizens toward their elected officials. On his return to the coast, he delayed in Washington where he spoke with officials of the State Department seeking to convince them to publish a guidebook for immigrants. He was even introduced to President Rutherford B. Hayes who seemed to have taken some interest in the cooperative movement. His tour, which had become a series of lecture appointments, was climaxed on November 15, 1879, when Holyoake delivered a lecture on coopera-tion to the students of Cornell University.[45]　He had indeed traveled a long distance since he had delivered his first lectures to the Worcester Socialists. From Ithaca, he went to New York City where, on November 18, he was honored with a public breakfast sponsored by cooperators and American freethinkers. The next day he sailed again for England. Very impressed with the possibilities the U.S. offered immigrants, Holyoake intended to present his conclusions to cooperators at home.

The British cooperative movement had become very firmly established in the ten years since the Cooperative Union had been formed. The Rochdale Pioneers had proved that a cooperative solution to economic difficulties was a workable possibility. Thou-sands of families were now in 1879 able to purchase goods at lower prices and thousands of workmen were employed by the manufac-turing cooperatives. These gains were hardly revolutionary, but they were nonetheless real. Holyoake also had achieved a measure of personal security which he had never before known. In 1880 no one would have believed that over a quarter century yet remained to Holyoake. Increasingly, as the ranks of his associates were thinned by death, Holyoake reflected on the past. As the end of the century drew near Holyoake became an object of veneration: a cooperative saint who had walked with Robert Owen. The days of being involved in the struggles of the working classes for economic and political advancement were over for Holyoake by 1880; the last years of his life were not, however, unproductive. He wrote constantly, he became an international ambassador for the Cooperative Union; and he was just active enough in liberal causes to preserve his spirit without destroying his fragile health.

NOTES TO CHAPTER SIX

[1] From the "Objects of the Rochdale Pioneers" recorded in Arnold Bonner's *British Cooperation* (Manchester: Cooperative Union Ltd., 1961), p. 46. See also G.D.H. Cole, *A Century of Cooperation* (London: George Allen and Unwin, Ltd., 1944).

[2] Cole, *A Century of Cooperation*, p. 81.

[3] Bonner, *British Cooperation*, p. 59.

[4] Sidney Pollard, "Nineteenth Century Cooperation: From Community Building to Shopkeeping," *Essays in Labour History*, ed. Asa Briggs and John Saville (New York: St. Martin's Press, 1967), pp. 95-102.

[5] *Ibid.*, p. 100.

[6] Holyoake, *The History of the Rochdale Pioneers*, 10th ed. (London: Swan Sonnenscheim and Company, 1893), p. 47.

[7] William Cooper, Secretary of the Pioneers, to Holyoake (March 11, 1858), No. 1005, C.U.

[8] *Westminster Review*, LXX (October, 1858), 576-77; the *Economist*, XVI, No. 770 (1858), 593; *New York Daily Tribune*, October 11, 1858.

[9] Holyoake, *History of the Rochdale Pioneers*, p. xi.

[10] Holyoake, *Moral Errors which Endanger the Permanence of Cooperative Societies* (Huddersfield: Henry Fielding, 1863), pp. 11-12.

[11] Holyoake, *A "Working Man's" Objections to Cooperative Societies Answered* (Huddersfield: Henry Fielding, 1863), p. 6.

[12] Walter Morrison to Holyoake (May 20, 1868), No. 1781 and (June 23, 1868), No. 1791, C.U. Also Holyoake to Morrison (May 23, 1868), No. 1784, C.U.

[13] *Social Economist*, No. 20 (October 1, 1868), p. 119.

[14] Cooperative Congress, *Proceedings*, I (1869), 86-88.

[15] *Ibid.*, 103-104.

[16] *Ibid.*, 86-87.

[17] *Ibid.*, II (1870), 20.

[18] Charles Bradlaugh and G.J. Holyoake, *Secularism, Scepticism, and Atheism* (London: Austin and Company, 1870).

[19] Bradlaugh to Holyoake (September 30, 1870), No. 1981, C.U.

[20] Holyoake to Charles Watts, one of Bradlaugh's closest disciples at this time. The letter is recorded in McCabe, *Life and Letters of Holyoake*, II, 57-58.

[21] *Reasoner*, XXX, No. 1 (1871), 13-14.

[22] McCabe, *Life and Letters of Holyoake*, II, 58-59.

[23] *Reasoner*, XXX, No. 1 (1871), 2.

[24] *Ibid.*, No. 3 (1871), 33. The *Reasoner* was being printed by the North of England Cooperative Printing Society.

[25] *Cooperative News*, I, No. 1 (1871), 1-2.

[26] Cooperative Congress, *Proceedings*, V, (1873), 51.

[27] Holyoake, *The Logic of Cooperation* (London: Trübner and Company, 1873), p. 6.

[28] Cooperative Congress, *Proceedings*, V, (1873), 54.

[29] Holyoake, *The Policy of Commercial Cooperation* (London: Trübner and Company, 1873), p. 10.

30 *Cooperative News*, III, No. 34 (1873), 417-18.

31 *Ibid.*, VI, No. 22 (1875), 261.

32 McCabe, *Life and Letters of Holyoake*, II, 103.

33 Holyoake, *The History of Cooperation* (London: T. Fisher Unwin, 1908), p. 159. Even though Holyoake received scathing condemnation by Jones who considered the statements slanderous, Holyoake refused to delete his satirical remarks from the later editions of the *History of Cooperation.*

34 *Cooperative News*, VI, No. 36 (1875), 426-27.

35 *Ibid.*, No. 48 (1875), 575.

36 *Secularist*, I, No. 1 (1876), 6.

37 *Ibid.*, No. 20 (1876), 314. These comments, directed against Foote, were reprinted from the *National Reformer.*

38 *Ibid.*, No. 24 (1876), 369-72.

39 *Secular Review and Secularist*, I, No. 9 (1877), 129.

40 G.H. Taylor quoted in Tribe, *One-Hundred Years of Free Thought,* p. 23.

41 *Cooperative News*, X, No. 8 (1879), 113.

42 For a complete account of his visit to the United States, see Holyoake, *Among the Americans* (Chicago: Belford, Clarke, and Company, 1881).

43 Robert Ingersoll to Holyoake (November 5, 1879), No. 2553, C.U.

44 *Cooperative News*, X, No. 42 (1879), 675.

45 *Ibid.*, No. 50 (1879), 813.

CHAPTER VII

TREADING FAMILIAR PATHS, 1880 — 1906

Owenism, Secularism, franchise reform and cooperation had served as successive foci around which Holyoake's life had revolved. In his later years, although he continued to be active until he died, Holyoake participated in no new major organization. It is possible, therefore, to narrate the affairs of his life after 1880 in a somewhat summary fashion because Holyoake was either engaged in familiar endeavors or in reflection upon his earlier activities.

Returning to England filled with enthusiasm for the United States, Holyoake energetically began to proclaim America as a land of opportunity awaiting the British emigrant. His experiences abroad had led him to adopt an almost utopian attitude. On February 7, 1880, for example, Holyoake addressed the Guild of Cooperators in London on the subject of emigration. In Great Britain, he explained, a surplus of labor existed. To those who found it difficult to obtain steady employment, emigration afforded a far greater range of opportunities:

> The new cry of progress is dispersion . . . Let those who have just employers honor them and continue in their service. Let all who can command adequate subsistence here remain and increase the honest renown and prosperity of their native land. But let the poor save a little capital at cooperative stores, and join the great fortune of those nations where freedom and equality dwell, and where wealth awaits all who have fortitude, common sense, courage and industry. [1]

Holyoake's proclamation was re-echoed by many during the last decades of the nineteenth century, especially when erratic business cycles and declining profits produced pockets of unemployment. Nearly four and one-half million residents of the British Isles departed for other lands—some to the United States, others to

149

Australia, Canada or New Zealand. Although he could hardly be labeled an imperialist, Holyoake was convinced that the sparsely inhabited areas of the world could absorb the excess population of European nations.

His 75th birthday found the elderly man in vigorous health. "Tho I was at work until 2 o'clock this morning," he noted, "I am as well as I ever was on a birthday."[2] Holyoake's efforts to facilitate emigration continued unabated by advancing years. He secured information from the U.S. Land Office about the procedures by which an immigrant could secure land. To the London Cooperative Guild, he offered over six hundred maps which he had obtained from the U.S. government of twenty-three states and two territories.[3] In 1882 Holyoake received £100 from the Public Service Fund to return to America and to continue his work on a guide book for emigrants. Accompanied by his daughter, Emilie, who did more than anyone to care for Holyoake in his later years, he again departed England for the United States in June 1882. This time he remained abroad for nearly five months, completing a journey that was astounding for one of his age and history of physical frailty. Holyoake's adventure carried him a distance of eight thousand miles by rail and stage coach as far west as Sante Fe and Las Vegas. Although he again failed to convince the U.S. government to publish a guidebook, the Canadians gave him a more favorable response and made one available.[4]

After his return to England in November 1882, Holyoake settled down to more mundane cooperative interests. He regularly attended meetings of the Southern section of the Cooperative Union until 1894; he assisted in a campaign to compel each producer cooperative to adopt a profit sharing plan; and on one occasion in 1887 he was invited to deliver the inaugural address to the annual cooperative congress—an honor usually reserved for a scholar, politician, or a ranking churchman.[5] He also became the unofficial ambassador of the British cooperators to their continental counterparts. British cooperators had always invited members of foreign cooperative organizations to their annual congresses and these favors were politely returned. In 1885 Holyoake visited the French cooperators in Paris; in 1886 and 1888, accompanied by E.V. Neale, he addressed the Italian cooperative congresses in Milan and Bologna where he was welcomed as a friend of Mazzini and Garibaldi.

Not only did he maintain his activity in the cooperative movement, but Holyoake also took part in a variety of political and liberal causes. From 1876 to 1884, Holyoake served with his old friend, C.D. Collet, on the Traveling Tax Abolition Committee which sought the removal of duties on third-class railway fares. In 1884 the Liberal government complied.[6] That same year Holyoake once again tried to win a seat in Parliament. The primary objective of his candidacy at Leicester, he relates in his autobiography, was to render support to Charles Bradlaugh. Bradlaugh had been sent to Parliament in 1880 by the electors of Northampton. He was, however, denied a seat on the grounds that, as an avowed atheist, he could not take the required oath.[7] Although the Prime Minister, William Gladstone, detested Bradlaugh's religious opinions, he supported the Affirmation Bill of 1883 because he believed that Bradlaugh's constitutional rights and those of the Northampton voters were being infringed. Public opinion on the question was against Bradlaugh, and the bill failed to secure a majority. Holyoake made it very clear in an unsuccessful attempt to win the endorsement of the Leicester Liberal Association that he supported Gladstone and the Liberals who had voted for affirmation.[8] In 1886 Parliament did finally allow Bradlaugh to be seated and two years later a permanent Affirmation Bill—a goal of the Secularists as early as the 1850s—became law.

Holyoake was indeed a most ardent supporter of the Liberal party. Holding a special admiration for Gladstone, Holyoake made quite certain that the Grand Old Man was sent copies of all his works. Upon receiving the *History of Cooperation* in 1875, Gladstone had expressed considerable interest and even invited Holyoake to breakfast in order that the two could more fully discuss cooperation. Unlike as their religious opinions were, Gladstone was nonetheless interested in the Secular idea, and he very much appreciated "the advantage of having it stated by sincere and high-minded men."[9] From the early 1880s until Gladstone's death in 1898, letters were regularly exchanged between the two men on political, religious and personal affairs. When Holyoake heard a rumor in 1881 that someone had memorialized Gladstone on his behalf for a pension, Holyoake wrote to discourage the idea on the grounds that he really was in no need of one.[10] Gladstone was impressed, responding immediately that Holyoake's letter had "heightened the respect and regard which I have felt for you ever since I have had the advantage of knowing you."[11] Holyoake did his best to cultivate the relationship and he succeeded. On September 1, 1884, Holyoake was present when Gladstone delivered a speech in Midlothian. "Its effect on English minds," he wrote praising the oration, "as I found in travelling home is very great—satisfying every sense of pride, justice, and conviction in the Liberal Party."[12] Their unwavering commitment to liberalism and mutual contempt for every form of intolerance, be it religious bigotry or political oppression, provided a basis for continuing communication.

In support of Gladstone's attempt to grant home rule to Ireland in 1886, Holyoake wrote *The Opportunity for Ireland*, a pamphlet in the National Liberal series. The same year he produced *Deliberate Liberalism*, an essay in which he delineated the tactical traps into which liberals were prone to fall. Although Holyoake considered liberalism superior to all other political positions because authority was derived from consent, he warned the Liberals that they must be more prepared to move from debate to action and that they also should be cognizant that law was the true basis of political freedom and social order. He asserted that serious difficulties arose

> when Liberals publicly contended that coercion in defense of order was alien to Liberalism, which meant that a Liberal is a sentimental fool who is prevented by his principles from coercing the man who would cut his throat. If it comes to be understood that freedom paralyses the hand of order, it would be a more serious argument against Liberty than tyranny ever invented. An intelligent Liberal is one who is for liberty of discussion till a question has been fully debated—then he comes to action. [13]

As Professor David Thomson of Cambridge has written, liberalism was the "operative political creed" of most Victorians. [14] In *Deliberate Liberalism*, Holyoake indicates that he had begun to perceive the dilemma which has historically plagued liberals when the consensus which permits free and rational discussion can no longer be achieved. Confronted by declining economic prosperity and rising Irish nationalism, the social unity which had allowed liberalism to mature had begun to fracture. To the end of his life, however, Holyoake supported the Liberal party, rejoicing in 1906 when they were again returned in the majority.

In addition to his later political essays, Holyoake produced numerous short tracts and books on cooperation and Secularism. Under Bradlaugh's leadership, the NSS had finally become a united cadre of freethinkers numbering about six thousand. Holyoake still retained the hope that Secularism could become a more popular creed if it were invested with broader and more positive aspirations. From 1883 to 1886 he edited the *Present Day*, a journal distributed to a very small number of readers, in which he expressed his opinions about issues facing the Secularists.

In 1896, exactly a half a century after he had first published the *Reasoner*, Holyoake produced his last book on Secularism. In *The Origin and Nature of Secularism* appeared all of his old claims about the positive nature of Secularism and duty to humanity. "Vindictiveness toward the erring," he wrote in a final plea for toleration, "is not only inconsistency, it is persecution."[15]   Characteristically, Holyoake dispatched a copy of the book to Gladstone who presented a rather thorough and sophisticated critique. Gladstone was convinced that Secularism was really a derivative of Christianity, its ethical emphasis "never would have existed without the Gospel."[16]   The greatest shortcoming of Secularism, Gladstone believed, was its materialism which forced adherents to surrender "to the cold embrace of extinction" the lives of "beautiful and noble characters." Obviously impressed by Gladstone's thoughtful reply, Holyoake acknowledged his own hope for an existence beyond the grave, stating that "my not being sure of it will not prevent it coming to me."[17]   This seems not to have been an idle statement for a year later when Gladstone was failing rapidly, Holyoake wrote, "For yourself I pray in my imperfect way that whatever you can wish may be given unto you . . . I often think of your last to me and conclude that belief like toleration is the growth of wider information which I seek as far as I am able."[18]

The aging Holyoake was still certain that Bradlaugh had misconceived the real essence of the movement. With characteristic good will he acknowledged, at the time of Bradlaugh's death in 1891, that his rival had "the distinction of accomplishing more than any man every did," for the freedom to hold minority opinions.[19] After all, an atheist in Parliament was testimony that some change had taken place in Victorian society's attitude toward its irreligious members. The Secularists had contributed to that change and, even though Holyoake detested Bradlaugh's flamboyant methods, he had to admit that Bradlaugh had brought attention to the issues. After Bradlaugh's death in 1891, the NSS continued to exist, a very select group reaching the general public chiefly through the tracts issued by the Rationalist Press Association founded in 1899. Although

Holyoake, for somewhat sentimental reasons, was elected the first chairman of the RPA, Charles Watts was the real founder of this society which included the rationalist historians Joseph McCabe and J.M. Robertson. [20]

During the early 1890s Holyoake did complete the major literary achievement of his life, his autobiography, *Sixty Years of an Agitator's Life*. It is indispensible for the study of Holyoake's career and it frequently appears in the bibliographies of political and social histories. Essentially, *Sixty Years* is a series of anecdotes, presented in general chronological order, about the significant events and the people—politicians, fellow radicals, and revolutionaries—whom Holyoake had known since his youth in Birmingham. It is hardly an example of revealing or introspective autobiography. We discover little of Holyoake's personality in its pages except the not very surprising fact that he considered himself to have been a good deal more influential than he really was. For example, Holyoake over-dramatized his relationship with European revolutionaries. Even with its shortcomings, however, the two volumes of *Sixty Years* are not dreary reading. Holyoake's light-heartedness served him well in print as it did on the speaker's platform. Filled with charming if not always historically accurate accounts and sketches, *Sixty Years* fascinated readers of the day and even now is delightful to read especially when compared with some of the more ponderous Victorian autobiographies.

The same measure of praise cannot be given his second venture in autobiography, *Bygones Worth Remembering*, published in 1905. Although Holyoake did have assistance, the volumes are haphazardly organized with much of the information being extracted verbatim from earlier works. *Bygones Worth Remembering* is, however, a suitable postscript to Holyoake's life for he did vigorously assert in 1905 that he had witnessed the winning of many earlier goals. "Changes in condition," he noted in the final pages, "are not estimated as they pass and when they have passed, many never look back to calculate their magnificence or insignificance." [21] Now, he observed, workingmen were better fed, housed, educated and enjoyed a generally higher standard of living than even the privileged contemporaries of their grandfathers. A political voice had been sought and gained. Holyoake was not unaware that the life of many a British laborer was routine and drab or that workers were still denied a minimum quality of existence. He was by no means an old romantic, sunken in nostalgic complacency. Confident that progress had been made, Holyoake believed that the "work of the day" would always remain.

The significant personal details of Holyoake's last years are few. In 1884 Eleanor Holyoake died in the forty-fifth year of her marriage to George Jacob. So little is recorded about Eleanor that one is forced to conclude that she accepted the lack of attention which her husband gave to family affairs with silent resignation. Holyoake conducted her funeral service himself, and C.D. Collet sang the same Secular hymn he had offered many years before at the graveside of little Max Holyoake. Two years later, in 1886, Holyoake remarried; about his second wife, Jane Pearson, nothing has been noted except that she did attend to the needs of an aged husband. After 1894 when illness again struck Holyoake, he became considerably less active, spending most of his time residing quietly in Brighton.

On January 22, 1906, after a few weeks of rapidly declining vitality, Holyoake died in the company of his second wife and his daughter, Emilie. He was buried in Highgate Cemetery, his simple funeral attended by thousands of cooperators and old friends. Draping his casket was an appropriate symbol of the English radical tradition: a Garibaldian flag. For cooperators, Holyoake's death signified the close of an important chapter in their history; the last of Owen's associates was now dead. Immediately upon his death, the Cooperative Union levied each member three pence for the construction of a suitable memorial. Today, Holyoake House in Manchester, the official headquarters of the Cooperative Union and the respository for his private papers, stands to the memory of George Jacob Holyoake.

*****

Without doubt the single most difficult task for the biographer is to portray accurately the dialogue between an individual and his times. The work is made the more difficult certainly in those instances where the subject of concern reveals little of his inner motivations. Holyoake was such a person; his letters, autobiographical work and the thousands of pages written for periodicals offer precious little foundation for judgments about the nature of the man. The documents do reveal Holyoake to have been temperate, honest, sincere and very tolerant. Even in his early years he presented his convictions with great restraint, carefully trying to avoid giving offense to those who could not share his beliefs. He was never unwilling to compromise and was always the first to condemn disorderly or irresponsible behavior. In his latter years, when the last generation of Victorians had grave doubts about the progress they were supposed to have made in the nineteenth century, Holyoake remained optimistic that the condition of the people of England would continue to improve. There are two final conclusions about Holyoake's life and his contribution to the Victorian age, I believe, which may be drawn with some degree of confidence.

For himself, Holyoake sought respectability more than any other personal goal. He certainly did believe it his duty to make a contribution to the progress of the working classes but his principal desire was to be recognized by his peers as a worthy person. At first glance it might seem almost inconceivable that any one who abjured Christianity and who frequently associated with agitators and revolutionaries could have attained any degree of acceptance into the mainstream of the Victorian world where the dominant value system conflicted so radically with many of Holyoake's basic beliefs. Yet it was possible. As diverse a group of people as Gladstone, the bigoted and patronizing Elcho, the skeptical Newman, and even the militant atheist and oft-times foe, Bradlaugh, admired Holyoake. Although his ideas were often indisputably radical, Holyoake's behavior was nearly always within the limits of accepted standards. Holyoake was indeed a radical but his actions were moderate.

Part of the explanation for Holyoake's achievement of respectability rests with his own desire for acceptance but the plain truth of the matter seems also to be that, after mid-century, many Victorians paid less concern to the ideas of those who challenged their society's dominant values and more attention to the mode by which such criticism was expressed. As R.C.K. Ensor has noted, the second generation of Victorians had become oriented more toward conduct than doctrine. [22] The evangelical discipline which had so greatly animated the first generation of Victorians had become secularized as respectability. Holyoake and other radicals thus acquired acceptance neither because their ideas had gained wide approval nor because they had greatly changed but because their conduct really disturbed so few people.

Holyoake's progress from an ostracized atheist in the 1840s to a respected spokesman for working class causes less than two decades later was a development paralleled generally in Victorian society after mid-century. Quite simply, the process of assimilation was at work. The industrial revolution had created a proletariat. And the radicalism expressed in the first half of the century by the unstamped press, Chartism and Owenism was the logical and painful cry of an exploited class. But working class protest was also prompted by the awareness of social isolation. The Chartists demanded to be brought within the pale of the constitution but the suffrage was to be more than an instrument of political power; it was to be a badge of their independence and social equality. The quest to create a true society was even more apparent in the activities of Owen and his disciples. After 1850, however, the political and economic forms of radicalism dissipated but not the basic goal of gaining recognition as legitimate members of society. Rather than seeking to gain respectability through massive agitation which had proven itself a failure or by asserting values which were so completely at variance with the middle class values which were coming to dominate Victorian society, new means had to be employed.

Although the concern for achieving political and economic inequality did not really diminish after 1850, the strong desire for personal improvement which had always been present among the working classes became more widely spread. And in the prosperous years after 1850, this personal advancement could be more easily gained thus making that goal appear even more realistic. The desire for personal improvement, the acceptance of the ideas of self-help, individualism—largely middle class objectives to be sure— were indeed internalized into the personality structures of large numbers of workingmen. [23] More than any other factor, this process produced the relative stability of mid-Victorian England. Holyoake and other moderate working class spokesmen performed a vitally important service in the process by which the urban working classes were integrated into Victorian culture.

The decline of ultra-radicalism in the third quarter of the nineteenth century has posed a difficult problem for historians of the British labor movement. The conclusion that economic prosperity was responsible for their comparative quietude is now accepted as a view far too narrow to explain the changes wrought in ideas and attitudes. [24] Class consciousness definitely did not disappear but it was indeed fractured and not until the last decades of the century would it be again clearly visible. But the period between the ultra-radical, utopian years and the later Victorian age, characterized by modern socialism and the drive for true labor representation in Parliament, was certainly one of true progress and was consistent with the basic goals of the laboring classes. Substantial numbers of working men and women, for good or ill depending on the bias of our own views, came to accept industrial society with its corresponding value system.

The success of assimilation, as it always does, depended upon communication. As a spokesman for the working classes, Holyoake reaffirmed to the other sectors of Victorian society that laboring men and women desired a true role and that they were willing to work peacefully and to be responsible for their actions. But more importantly, Holyoake was a spokesman to the working classes. He never lost his class consciousness even in later years. Beginning with his first attempt in the early 1840s as an Owenite missionary and continuing to his last years as a staunch supporter of the Liberal party, Holyoake sought to educate the working classes to those standards of conduct which were loudly proclaimed from platform, pulpit and press. To be literate and capable of reason, to provide for one's self and family, to act responsibly and independently, and to vote were the criteria by which the Victorians believed the worth of one another should be judged. By presenting these values to the working class in a form which they could accept, George Jacob Holyoake won respectability for himself and a large measure of progress for the classes with whom he identified.

NOTES TO CHAPTER SEVEN

1 *Cooperative News*, XI, No. 7 (1880), 98.

2 Holyoake to Eleanor Holyoake (April 13, 1882), No. 2702, C.U.

3 *Cooperative News*, XI, No. 27 (1880), 446.

4 See Holyoake, *Travels in Search of a Settler's Guide Book of America and Canada* (London: Trubner and Company, 1884).

5 E.V. Neale to Holyoake (April 1, 1887), No. 3078, C.U.

6 McCabe, *Life and Letters of Holyoake*, II, 151.

7 Holyoake, *Sixty Years*, II, 562-64.

8 Holyoake to Leicester Liberal Association (1884), No. 2922, C.U.

9 W.E. Gladstone to Holyoake (August 3, 1875), No. 2320, C.U.

10 Holyoake to Gladstone (March 11, 1881), No. 2628, C.U.

11 Gladstone to Holyoake (March 12, 1881), No. 2630, C.U.

12 Holyoake to Gladstone (September 2, 1884), No. 2949, C.U.

13 Holyoake, *Deliberate Liberalism* (London: John Heywood, 1886), p. 4.

14 David Thomson, *England in the Nineteenth Century* (Baltimore: Penguin Books, 1950), p. 224.

15 Holyoake, *The Origin and Nature of Secularism* (London: Watts and Company, 1896), p. 16.

16 Gladstone to Holyoake (January 11, 1897), No. 3590, C.U.

17 Holyoake to Gladstone (January 14, 1897), No. 3592, C.U.

18 Holyoake to Gladstone (March 3, 1898), No. 3653, C.U.

19 General Committee for Centennial Celebration, *Champion of Liberty: Charles Bradlaugh* (London: Watts and Company, 1933), p. 74.

20 See A.G. Whyte, *The Story of the RPA* (London: Watts and Company, 1949).

21 Holyoake, *Bygones Worth Remembering* (London: T. Fisher Unwin, 1905), II, 280.

22 R.C.K. Ensor, *England, 1870-1914* (Oxford: The Clarendon Press, 1936), p. 137.

23 Trygve R. Tholfsen, "The Intellectual Origins of Mid-Victorian Stability," *The Political Science Quarterly*, LXXXVI, No. 1 (March, 1971), 61.

24 See John Saville's introduction to Gammage, *History of the Chartist Movement*, pp. 42-45.

APPENDIX 1

APPENDIX 1

FINANCIAL TABLE OF TWENTY VOLUMES OF THE 'REASONER.' [1]

Number of the Volume	Printing Expenses (£ s. d.)	Total Proceeds (£ s. d.)	Deficiency of Printing Expenses (£ s. d.)	Surplus of Printing Expenses (£ s. d.)	Propagandist Fund (£ s. d.)	Paid to Fleet St. House From Propagandist Fund (£ s. d.)	Editor's Salary (£ s. d.)	Editor's Loss (£ s. d.)	Nos. in Each Vol	Price of Each No.
I.	199 4 6	159 11 6½	39 12 11½		38 1 4			1 11 7½	26	2d. & 1½d.
II.	114 18 6	125 6 4½		10 7 10¼	28 19 8		39 7 6¼		26	1½ d. & 2d.
III.	144 12 0	153 12 6	9 0 6		50 0 0		59 0 6		26	2d.
IV.	157 5 0	133 4 7	24 0 5		50 0 0		25 19 7		26	2d.
V.	167 3 6	151 17 3	15 6 3		46 7 0		31 0 9		31	2d.
VI.	144 12 6	119 6 8½	25 5 9½		35 8 9		10 3 0		26	2d.
VII.	126 19 0	128 8 0		1 9 0	33 1 9		34 10 9		27	1d.
VIII.	60 4 6	47 4 8	12 19 10		36 10 0		23 10 2		13	1d.
IX.	230 14 6	164 7 8	66 6 10		50 16 10			15 10 0	26	1d.
X.	273 6 3	204 2 6	69 3 9		97 10 0		28 6 3		32	1d.
XI.	223 11 0	192 10 6	31 0 6		51 15 0		20 14 6		26	1d.
XII.	274 9 0	215 16 11½	58 8 3½		42 7 7			16 0 8½	30	1d.
XIII.	233 5 3	222 11 1½	10 17 10½		25 3 8		14 5 9½		29	1d.
XIV.	313 5 0	282 12 0	30 13 0		45 17 2		15 14 2		26	1d.
XV.	337 6 6	312 9 9	24 16 9		166 4 4		11 7 5		26	1d.
XVI.	326 7 0	300 0 0	26 7 0		33 9 6		139 13 6		26	1d.
XVII.	289 16 0	288 0 0	1 16 0		95 18 2	41 0 0	31 13 2		27	1d. & 1½d.
XVIII.	133 2 0	147 7 0		14 5 0	57 3 4		69 3 1		12	1½d. & 2d.
XIX.	605 8 6	601 14 3	3 14 3				53 9 1		40	2d.
XX.	325 8 6	327 2 6		1 14 0	197 19 11	150 0 0	49 13 11		26	2d.

[1] G.J. Holyoake, *The History of Fleet Street House* (London: Holyoake and Company, 1856), p. 9.

APPENDIX 2

APPENDIX 1

APPENDIX 2

TRUTHS TO TEACH

1. To teach that the Churches, in affirming the existence of a Being independent of Nature, affirm what they do not know themselves—that they who say that they have discovered Deity assume to have found out what he has evidently chosen to conceal from men in this life by endowing them only with finite powers—that while the science of theology (if such it may be called) can only assure us that Deity *is*, without being able to tell us *what* he is, or how he exists, can be nothing more than a science of conjecture—that whoever bids us depend upon the fruition of a future life may betray us from the well use of this world—and whoever teaches us that the special help of Providence is available in this life, does betray men more or less to their own destruction.

2. To teach men to limit, therefore as a matter of truth and certainty, their affirmations to what they know—to restrict, as a matter of self-defense, their expectations to that which their experience warrants.

3. To teach men to see that the sum of all knowledge and duty is secular—that it pertains to this world alone.

4. To teach men to see that morality has an independent origin—that it has natural sanctions of the most effective kind, and that men may deduce their course of life and behavior from that which their real nature points out.

5. To teach men to trust Reason throughout, and to trust nothing that Reason does not establish—to examine all things hopeful, respect all things probable, but *rely* upon nothing which does not come within the range of phenomena, or of common consciousness, or assumes the form of law.

6. To teach men that the universal free, fair, and open discussion of opinion is the highest test of vital truth—that only that theory which is submitted to that ordeal is to be regarded, as only that which endures it can be trusted—that the discussion of opinion is therefore our interest, and to promote its utterance on the part of others a duty.

G.J.H.

APPENDIX 3

APPENDIX 3

CONSTITUTION AND OBJECTS OF SECULAR SOCIETIES
MANCHESTER 1852

Preamble of the Secular Socieites—The purpose of these societies is to render service to mankind, and the protection of the members against the practical consequences of speculative errors. But first service, and afterwards self-defense.

No programme of reformation will be successful in this day which does not create the conviction that its issues are Reason, Concert, and Progress.

Reason, which guarantees dispassionate action, free from the prostration of Superstition and the anarchy of Individualism.

Concert, the capacity to act with others—an earnest of goodwill to all.

Progress, the word of hope to the miserable, and of intelligent security to the contented.

Definition of Secularism—Secularism is the philosophy of the things of time. A secular is one who gives primary attention to those subjects, the issues of which can be tested by human experience. The secular principle requires that *precedence* be given to the duties of this life over those which pertain to another world.

Operations of the Societies
I.   The dissemination of positive principle corrective of spiritual error.
II. Devising secular plans for the improvement of local condition.
III. Defense of secular principle against whatever contradicts it, in moral respects, or impedes temporal progress.

Objects of the Secular Societies
I.   To promote primary attention to secular subjects.
II. To teach that Science is the providence of Life, and to warn men that absolute spiritual dependency in human affairs may involve material destruction.
III. The inculcation of Morals independently of Revealed Religion, by basing them on secular considerations more immediate, more demonstrative, and universal than those furnished by Scriptural Theology.

Chief Officers—The Chief officers of each society shall be a Director and a Secretary, who shall be elected, or re-elected by the members in January and, if possible, paid a salary for their services, which services the society should feel free to command.

Character of Officers—A merely theoretical society is an affair of the closet; to be an element in daily life, a society must exercise personal influence. To this end its members must be not only even-handed, but clean-handed. To affect a special morality would be purism and impertinence, but the officers of the society should be the persons against whom the world can sustain no serious charge of moral offense.

Rule of Moral Judgment—Not, however, to make ourselves the slave of any code of factitious and conventional morality which narrow sectaries may set up, which would preclude progress, we hold that 'no man or woman is accountable to others for any conduct by which others are not injured or damaged,' and we will recognize no allegations included in this rule. Our standard of moral judgment must be so far self chosen and not imposed upon us by opponents.

(Next follow procedural instructions)

Qualifications of Members—Each member should possess some working efficiency, or be willing to acquire it. To be able to explain his views by tongue or pen, to observe carefully, to report judiciously, to reason dispassionately, are desirable accomplishments for the Propagandist. Each society will endeavor to provide instruction in these arts, or point out opportunities of acquiring such knowledge—opportunities which members may be able to embrace.

Duties of Members—The duties assigned to each member should be such as are within his means, as respects power and opportunity; such indeed, as interfere neither with his social nor civil obligations; the intention being that the membership of the society shall not be incompatible with the preservation of health, and the primary service due to family and state.

Conditions of Federation—Any persons, wherever situated, acquainted with the 'Constitution and Objects of the Secular Societies,' (etc.) shall be recognized as a Secular Society.

Advantages of Secular Alliance—The advocacy of secularism has recast the policy and purport of freethinking—has developed its positive side—divested it of personal antagonism and indiscriminate disparagement. It has created for freethinking a better acceptation with the public and the Churches than heretofore; and those may avail themselves of the advantages of a new influence who can confederate with the Secular Societies.

Rule of Controversy—To institute any societies in the old spirit of indiscriminate disparagement of bodies, or antagonism of persons, would be futile . . . Such disparagements as are included in the explicit condemnation of erroneous principles are, we believe, all that the public defense of opinion requires, and are the kind of disparagement we propose to employ.

Local Exertions—Wherever a society exists, the first inquiry should be into the special work to be done in that neighborhood. Where a special error requires to be combatted, or some erroneous impression to be corrected, a paper upon it will be prepared in this wise. The subject being stated, each person will give his opinion on it. After this suggestive discussion, papers will be prepared and read at another assembly, and the best paper chosen. The most useful ideas in other papers will be placed at the service of the successful writer, the paper published, and the writer remunerated for its production. Such paper or tract will become one of the transactions of the society.

Lectures—If possible, a weekly lecture will be given publicly, under the authority of the society . . .

Schools—Efforts must be made for the institution of Secular Day and Sunday Schools in connection with every society. The Sunday School in the summer school should be held in the fields.

Suggestions to Societites—The members of each society may perhaps advantageously be limited to that number which admits of efficient communication . . . In the appointment of duties, some members may be charged with the care of the places of assembly, and all that relates thereto . . . Some may report the nature of all new works which are known to have relation to us . . . Some may attend special pulpits and controversial lectures . . . Others may have charge of the Church newspapers—others the Catholic organs—others the Dissenting—others the Sunday School publications, the Religious tract society, the reviews.

General Propagandist Fund—Once a year, in January, each Society shall collect and transmit to the Central Council, a contribution equivalent to one half-penny per week for each member, The said contributions shall be acknowledged and accounted for in *The Reasoner.*

Independence of Societies—It being intended to conserve as much individual independence as possible, each society will be held free to devise its own local regulations not herein specified, which are purposely kept few in general.

Conference and Council—A Conference of Delegates from each Secular Society shall, if possible, be held in some principal town in October in each year. Each society of more than forty members may send two delegates. The Central Council, elected by the conference, shall elect the Central Director and Secretary.

SELECT BIBLIOGRAPHY

SELECT BIBLIOGRAPHY

I. Primary Materials
  A. Manuscript Collections
   1. Bishopsgate Institute, London. *The Holyoake Collection.*
   2. Early correspondence, Log Books, and Diaries of G.J. Holyoake.
   3. The Cooperative Union Ltd., Manchester, *The Holyoake Collection.*
  B. A select list of the published writings of G.J. Holyoake (includes works edited by Holyoake)
   The Advantages and Disadvantages of Trades Unions. Sheffield: Hardcastle, 1841.
   Among the Americans. Chicago: Belford, Clarke and Company, 1881.
   Bygones Worth Remembering. London: T. Fisher Unwin, 1905.
   Deliberate Liberalism. London: John Heywood, 1886.
   The History of Cooperation. London: T. Fisher Unwin, 1908. The first volume was published in 1875 by Trübner; the second, also by Trubner, appeared in 1879. A complete edition was first published by T. Fisher Unwin in 1906.
   The History of Fleet Street House. London: Holyoake and Company, 1856.
   History of the Last Trial by Jury for Atheism in England. London: James Watson, 1850.
   The History of the Rochdale Pioneers. London: Swan Sonnenscheim and Company, 1893. (This is the tenth edition of *Self-Help by the People*, published in 1858.)
   The Liberal Situation: Necessity for a Qualified Franchise. London: The London Bookstore, 1865.
   The Logic of Cooperation. London: Trübner and Company, 1873.
   The Logic of Death. London: James Watson, 1850.
   The Movement. 1843-1845.
   Moral Errors which Endanger the Permanence of Co-operative Societies. Huddersfield: H. Fielding, 1863.
   A New Defence of the Ballot. London: Bookstore, 1868.
   The Opportunity for Ireland. London: N.L.C., 1886.
   Oracle of Reason. 1841-1843.
   The Origin and Nature of Secularism. London: Watts and Company, 1896. An American edition was also published, *English Secularism.* Chicago: Open Court Publishing Company, 1896.
   Paley Refuted in His Own Words. London: Hetherington, 1843.
   The Policy of Commercial Cooperation. London: Trübner and Company, 1873.
   Practical Grammar. London: Watson, 1844.
   Principles of Secularism. Holyoake and Company, 1859.
   Rationalism: A Treatise for the Times. London: James Watson, 1846.

Reasoner. 1846-1861, 1871-1872.

Secularist. 1876.

A Short and Easy Method With the Saints. London: Hetherington, 1843.

Sixty Years of an Agitator's Life. London: T. Fisher Unwin, 1892.

Social Economist. 1868-1869.

Travels in Search of a Settler's Guide Book of American and Canada. London: Trübner and Company, 1884.

The Trial of Theism. London: Holyoake and Company, 1857.

Utilitarian Record. 1846-1848.

A Visit to Harmony Hall. London: Hetherington, 1844.

Working Class Representation: Its Conditions and Consequences. Birmingham: Guest, 1868.

The Working Man. 1866.

A "Working Man's" Objections to Cooperative Societies Answered. Huddersfield: H. Fielding, 1863.

The Workman and the Suffrage. London: Holyoake and Company, 1859.

Holyoake, G.J. and Rutherford, J.H. *Christianity vs. Secularism.* Ward and Co., 1854.

C. Other Primary Materials

Anti-Persecution Union. *The Trial of George Jacob Holyoake on an Indictment of Blasphemy.* London: T. Paterson, 1842.

Barker, Joseph. *The Abominations of Socialism Exposed.* Newcastle: J. Blackwell and Co., 1840.

Bonner, Hypatia Bradlaugh, and Robertson, J.M. *Charles Bradlaugh.* London: T. Fisher Unwin, 1895.

Bradlaugh, Charles, and Holyoake, G.J. *Secularism, Scepticism, and Atheism.* London: Austin and Company, 1870.

Carpenter, William. *The Trial of Charles Southwell for Blasphemy.* London: Hetherington, 1842.

The Christian Socialist. 1850-1851.

Collet, Charles D. *History of the Taxes on Knowledge.* London: T. Fisher Unwin, 1899.

Comte, Auguste. *The Positive Philosophy.* Translated by Harriet Martineau. London: John Chapman, 1853.

Cooperative Congress. *Proceedings of Annual Congresses.* 1869-1880.

Cooperative News. 1871-1882.

The Economist, XVI, No. 770 (May 29, 1858), 593.

Great Britain. Hansard's Parliamentary Debates. LI (1840), 510-32.

Great Britain. Sessional Papers, Vol. LXXXIX *(Reports).* December, 1853.

London Quarterly Review, I, No. 1 (September, 1853), 146-49.

National Reformer. January - April, 1862.

A Narrative of Circumstances Connected with the Confinement of Dr. Robert Reid Kalley. London: J. Hatchard and Son, 1844.

New Moral World. 1839-1845.

Pearson, Thomas. *Infidelity, its Aspects, Causes, and Agencies.* New York: Robert Carter and Bros., 1854.

"Religious Heresies of the Working Class," *Westminster Review,* n.s. XXI (January - April, 1862), 60-97.

Report of a Public Discussion Between Reverend Brewin Grant and George Jacob Holyoake. London: Ward and Company, 1853.

Secular Review and Secularist. 1877.

Smiles, Samuel. *Self-Help.* London: John Murray, 1958. This edition, edited by Asa Briggs, is the centenary edition of Smiles's original work.

Southwell, Charles. *Socialism Made Easy.* London: James Watson, 1840.

The Times (London), 1852, 1866.

Walpole, S.W. *The History of Twenty-Five Years.* London: Longmans, Geen and Company, 1904.

Westminster Review, n.s. IV (July - October, 1853), 246-48; and LXX (October 1858), 576-77.

II. Secondary Works

Anderson, Olive. *A Liberal State at War.* New York: St. Martin's Press, 1967.

Arnstein, Walter. *The Bradlaugh Case.* Oxford: The Clarendon Press, 1965.

Armytage, W.H.G. *Heavens Below: Utopian Experiments in England, 1560-1960.* Toronto: University of Toronto Press, 1961.

Armytage, W.H.G. and Mack, Edward. *Thomas Hughes.* London: Ernest Benn, Ltd., 1952.

Ausubel, Herman. *John Bright: Victorian Reformer.* New York: John Wiley and Sons, Inc., 1966.

Backstrom, Philip. *Christian Socialism and Cooperation in Victorian England.* London: Croom Helm, Ltd., 1974.

Bellamy, Joyce M. and Saville, John (eds.) *Dictionary of Labour Biography.* Volume I. London: MacMillan & Co., Ltd., 1972.

Blake, Robert. *Disraeli.* New York: Doubleday and Company, 1968.

Bonner, Arnold. *British Cooperation.* Manchester: Cooperative Union, Ltd., 1961.

Briggs, Asa. "The Background of the Parliamentary Reform Movement in Three English Cities (1830-1832)," *Cambridge Historical Journal,* X (1952), 293-317.

_____. *The Making of Modern England, 1783-1867.* New York: Harper and Row, Publishers, 1965.

_____. "Social Structure and Politics in Birmingham and Lyons (1835-1848)," *British Journal of Sociology,* I (March, 1950), 67-80.

_____. *Victorian People*. New York: Harper and Row, Publishers, 1963.

Briggs, Asa (ed.) *Chartist Studies*. London: MacMillan and Company, Ltd., 1960.

_____ and Saville, John, *Essays in Labour History*. London: MacMillan and Company, Ltd., 1967.

Bury, J.B. *A History of the Freedom of Thought*. London: Oxford University Press, 1952.

Christensen, Torban. "Origin and History of Christian Socialism," *Acta Theologica Danica*, III (1962).

Cole, G.D.H. *British Working Class Politics, 1832-1914*. London: The Labor Book Service, 1914.

_____. *A Century of Cooperation*. London: George Allen and Unwin, Ltd., 1944.

Cowling, Maurice. *1867: Disraeli, Gladstone and Revolution*. Cambridge: University Press, 1967.

Davies, G.C.B. *Henry Philpotts, Bishop of Exeter*. London: S.P.C.K., 1954.

Ensor, R.C.K. *England, 1870-1914*. Oxford: The Clarendon Press, 1936.

Eros, John. "The Rise of Organized Free Thought in Mid-Victorian Britain," *The Sociological Review*, II (July, 1954), 98-120.

Gammage, R.G. *History of the Chartist Movement*. New York: Augustus M. Kelley Publishers, 1969. (Originally published by Holyoake and Company, 1854.)

Gill, Conrad. *History of Birmingham*. London: Oxford Unaiversity Press, 1952.

Gillespie, C.C. *Genesis and Geology*. New York: Harper and Row, Publishers, 1959.

Gillespie, Frances E. *Labor and Politics in England, 1850-1867*. Durham, N.C.: Duke University Press, 1927.

Goss, C.W.F. *A Contribution Towards a Bibliography of the Writings of George Jacob Holyoake*. London: Watts and Company, 1908. This short work was appended to Joseph McCabe's *Life and Letters of George Jacob Holyoake*. Later, it was published as a separate book.

Harrison, J.F.C. *Quest for the New Moral World*. New York: Charles Scribner's Sons, 1969.

_____. *Learning and Living, 1790-1960*. Toronto: The University of Toronto Press, 1961.

Harrison, Royden, *Before the Socialists*. London: Routledge and Keagan Paul, 1965.

_____. "The British Working Class and the General Election of 1868," *International Review of Social History*, VI (1961)

Hobsbawm, E.J. *Labouring Men*. New York: Doubleday and Company, 1964.

Houghton, Walter. *The Victorian Frame of Mind*. New Haven: Yale University Press, 1957.

Inglis, K.S. *Churches and the Working Class in Victorian*

England. Toronto: University of Toronto Press, 1963.

_____. "Patterns of Religious Worship in 1851," *Journal of Ecclesiastical History*, XI (April, 1960), 74-86.

Kitchel, Anna Theresa. *George Lewes and George Eliot.* New York: The John Day Company, 1933.

Kitson-Clark, G. *The Making of Victorian England.* New York: Atheneum, 1967.

Maccoby, Simon. *English Radicalism, 1853-1886.* London: George Allen and Unwin, Ltd., 1938.

Magnus, Philip. *Gladstone.* New York: E.P. Dutton and Company. 1964.

Marty, Martin. *The Modern Schism.* New York: Harper and Row, Publishers, 1969.

Maruice, Frederick (ed.). *The Life of F.D. Maurice.* New York: Charles Scribner's Sons, 1884.

McCabe, Joseph. *The Life and Letters of George Jacob Holyoake.* London: Watts and Company, 1908.

Miliband, Ralph. "The Politics of Robert Owen," *Journal of the History of Ideas*, XV (April, 1954), 233-245.

Orr, Edwin. *The Second Evangelical Awakening.* London: Marshall, Morgan and Scott, Ltd., 1949.

Packe, Michael St. John *Orsini.* Boston: Little, Brown and Company, 1957.

Park, Joseph. *The English Reform Bill of 1867.* New York: Columbia University Press, 1920.

Podmore, Frank. *Robert Owen.* New York: D. Appleton and Company, 1907.

Pollard, Sidney and Salt, John (eds.) *Robert Owen: Prophet of the Poor.* London: MacMillan Press, Ltd., 1971.

Raven, C.W. *Christian Socialism, 1848-1854.* London: MacMillan and Company, Ltd., 1920.

Robertson, J.M. *A History of Freethought in the Nineteenth Century.* London: Watts and Company, 1929.

Robson, Robert (ed.) *Ideas and Institutions of Victorian Britain.* London: G. Bell and Sons, Ltd., 1967.

Rosenblatt, Frank. *The Social and Economic Aspects of the Chartist Movement.* New York: Columbia University Press, 1916.

Royle, Edward. "George Jacob Holyoake and the Secularist Movement in Britain." Unpublished Dissertation, Cambridge University, 1968.

_____. "Mechanics Institutes and the Working Classes, 1840-1860," *The Historical Journal,* XIV (1971), 305-320.

_____. *Victorian Infidels; The origins of the British Secularist Movement,* 1791-1866 (Totowa; Rowman & Littlefield, 1974).

Saville, John (ed.). *Democracy and the Labour Movement.* London: Laurence and Wishart, Ltd., 1954.

Sheldon, Henry. *Unbelief in the Nineteenth Century.* New York: Eaton and Mains, 1907.

Simon, Walter, *European Positivism in the Nineteenth Century.* Ithaca, New York: Cornell University Press, 1963.

Slossen, Preston William. *The Decline of the Chartist Movement.* New York: Columbia University Press, 1916.

Smith, F.B. *The Making of the Second Reform Bill.* Cambridge: University Press, 1966.

Stern, Fritz (ed.) *The Varieties of History.* Cleveland: World Publishing Company, 1956.

Tholfsen, Trygve. "The Intellectual Origins of Mid-Victorian Stability," *The Political Science Quarterly,* LXXXVI, No. 1 (March, 1971).

Thompson, E.P. *The Making of the English Working Class.* New York: Vintage Books, 1963.

Thomson, David. *England in the Nineteenth Century.* Baltimore: Penguin Books, 1950.

Trevelyan, George Macauley. *The Life of John Bright.* London: Constable and Company, Ltd., 1913.

Tribe, David. *One Hundred Years of Free Thought.* London: Elek Books, Ltd., 1967.

Tylecote, Mabel. *The Mechanics' Institutes of Lancashire and Yorkshire Before 1851.* Manchester: The University Press, 1957.

Vincent, John. *The Formation of the British Liberal Party.* New York: Charles Scribner's Sons, 1966.

Webb, R.K. *The British Working Class Reader, 1790-1848.* London: George Allen and Unwin, Ltd., 1955.

_____. *Harriet Martineau, a Radical Victorian.* London: Heinemann, 1960.

Whyte, A.G. *The Story of the R.P.A.* London: Watts and Company, 1949.

Wood, Anthony. *Nineteenth Century Britain.* London: McKay, 1960.

Woodward, Llewellyn. *The Age of Reform.* Oxford: The Clarendon Press, 1962.

INDEX

INDEX